"The woman of today is bombarded and confused by so many false-hoods. These messages may originate from painful childhood experiences or from media that emphasize beauty and glitz above all else. Or perhaps from a culture that tells women their role as a wife and mother doesn't count nearly as much as a career. Or the more selfish trend is that if her marriage doesn't make her happy, she owes it to herself to bail out. In *Lies Women Believe: And the Truth that Sets Them Free* Nancy Leigh DeMoss exposes Satan as the source of these falsehoods and points women back to the truth found only in God's Word. Whatever problem today's woman may face—guilt, addictions, an unhappy marriage, desire for career over mothering children, troubled children, the list goes on—she reminds us that there is an answer, and it is found in God. God is enough."

TIM AND BEVERLY LaHAYE

"Nancy Leigh DeMoss, who is one of the most articulate Bible expositors in the Christian world today, has written a book that I hope will get to the top of the bestseller list. It exposes the lies that imprison so many women and sets them free. I highly recommend it."

CHARLES COLSON

"For a quarter of a century, Nancy Leigh DeMoss has listened compassionately to heart-wrenching stories about the ways women in today's world are looking for meaning in life in all the wrong places. Readers will find themselves in these stories.

"A careful reading of this compelling book, written by someone who knows and loves the Scriptures, will help women identify and break out of the many bondages—emotional, physical and spiritual—that trap them. It will also lead women to a new vision for their lives, and the profound sense of freedom that comes with the knowledge of God's redeeming love made known in Jesus Christ.

"Nancy's breathtaking book arrives on the American scene at a timely moment in history, when the populace is confused, desperately searching for meaning in life, and buying into anything that brings immediate gratification. This liberating book will be a blessing to you."

GEORGE AND KINGSLEY GALLUP

"What a timely, God-initiated and God-endorsed book! Nancy is a friend not only to us and to our family, but to thousands who have heard her speak and have known her personally. This is a most timely and crucial contribution to all women. Nancy deals honestly with the most pressing pain in women's lives and shows sensitively real illustrations and the truth that sets them free. Without hesitation, we encourage every woman to carefully study and apply this wonderful and practical spiritual help—both hurting and bewildered women, as well as radiant and happy women who desire to help others."

HENRY AND MARILYN BLACKABY

"Have you ever wished you had a trusted friend, a wise counselor, that you could go to for godly, profoundly biblical advice? Someone you could go to who would help you tackle life's thorniest questions? Nancy Leigh DeMoss may not be your closest friend, but she will provide you with the solid Psalm 1 counsel that your soul longs for. On more than one occasion we've sought Nancy's advice and counsel. She is a godly woman with a heart for God's people. Compassionate and caring, I think you'll find that Nancy will stimulate you to love and good deeds in these pages. Buy two of these books—one for yourself and one for your best friend!"

DENNIS AND BARBARA RAINEY

"Finally we can stop walking around in a maze of unanswered questions. The 'why's' have been silenced and the truth proclaimed! Nancy penetrates the confusion of our day and helps us see through the deception that has plunged so many women into despair and frustration. Then she gently leads us into the truth that is the only pathway to experience God's beautiful peace and restoration."

P. BUNNY WILSON

"Today's women need to hear the truth, and I praise God for Nancy Leigh DeMoss' incredible faith in His truth and her honesty about our weakness. She refuses to compromise His Word for the world's sake."

HEATHER WHITESTONE MCCALLUM
Miss America 1995

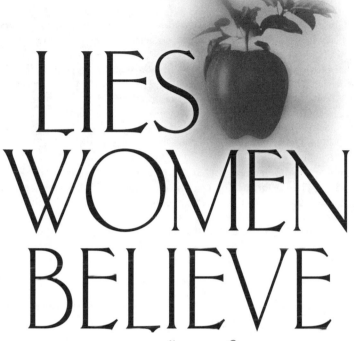

LIES
WOMEN
BELIEVE

and the
TRUTH THAT
SETS THEM FREE

*N*ancy Leigh DeMoss

MOODY PRESS
CHICAGO

The women's testimonies and stories in this book are true. Unless both the first and last name are given, names of women and minor details of their stories have been changed to maintain anonymity.

Library of Congress Cataloging-in-Publication Data

DeMoss, Nancy Leigh.
   Lies women believe and the truth that sets them free / Nancy Leigh DeMoss ; foreword by Elisabeth Elliot.
      p. cm.
   Includes bibliographical references.
   ISBN 0-8024-7296-6
   1. Christian women--Religious life. I. Title.

BV4527 .D46 2001
248.8'43--dc21

00-068110

To my mother

who taught me to recognize
many of the lies women believe
and who knows the importance and power
of the Truth

❧ CONTENTS ❧

✤ SECTION THREE: WALKING IN THE TRUTH

✂ ACKNOWLEDGMENTS ✂

As with any major undertaking, this book has been a team effort. I am indebted to many dear friends and colleagues who have labored with me to give birth to this message. Among them, I offer special gratitude to:

The Moody Press team—what a joy it has been to work together. You were the first to have the vision for publishing this message. Without your encouragement, this book might never have been written. And thank you, Anne Scherich, for your help with those last-minute touch-ups.

Lela Gilbert—you are a kindred spirit. Thank you for modeling a courageous commitment to walk in the Truth, and for helping me think through and express some of these difficult issues that are on both our hearts.

Dr. Bruce Ware—your love for the Truth is infectious. I am grateful for the spiritual covering and protection the Lord provided me through your careful, theological review and your enormously helpful input.

Becca Craven, Del and Debra Fehsenfeld, Sandra Hawkins, Janet Johnson, and Monica Vaught—thank you for lifting up my hands in so many ways, including providing research assistance and/or making suggestions on the manuscript. Your help has been vital.

Life Action Ministries staff wives—I've lost track of the number of times you have sent encouraging notes or voice-mail messages, stopped to ask how it was going, or delivered home-cooked meals while I was writing in seclusion. Your lives adorn the Gospel and reflect the beauty of the Truth.

My dear "praying friends"—how blessed I am to have you "keeping watch" over my soul. Thank you for surrounding and undergirding me in the midst of the battle. Your prayers have given me courage and helped me stay faithful to the Truth.

Finally—eternity will not be long enough to express my gratitude to You, Lord Jesus. You are the Truth that has set me free, and I love You with all my heart!

❧ FOREWORD ❦

Nancy Leigh DeMoss, a woman of compassion and keen insight, has had the courage to plumb the depths of women's illusions and delusions, of their hopes, fears, failures, and sorrows, so much of which might have been avoided were it not for lies propagated thirty or more years ago—such as "You can have it all," "Don't get caught in the compassion trap," "Anything men can do we can do better," etc.

But of course the lies began long before that. The woman God gave to the first man, Adam, listened to the Whisperer: *Hath God said?* Eve listened to the snake in the garden. Then, instead of protecting her from the lies being propagated, her husband said, in effect, "If this is what the little lady wants, this is what the little lady should have." Consequently, sin entered into the world and death by sin. Eve refused what was given, usurped what was not given, and said, in effect, *"My will be done."*

Thanks be to God, there is redemption. A humble village girl in Nazareth was visited by an angel, who delivered a startling message. Mary was to become the mother of the Son of God. Although she was greatly troubled, she received the message. "I am the Lord's servant," she responded. "May it be to me as you have said."

It is my prayer that the Spirit of God will direct you as you read this greatly needed book. "The essence of true salvation," the author writes, "is not a matter of profession or performance; rather it is a transformation: 'If anyone is in Christ, he is a new creation; the old has gone, the new has come!'"

ELISABETH ELLIOT

❧ INTRODUCTION ❧

B anished from Eden, wearing clothes of animal skins, her husband sore at her, and on her way to being the mother of the first murdered child—and the mother of his killer—Eve must have felt very low.

Alone.

Defeated.

A failure.

How hard it must have been to walk with Adam east of Eden into a world in which it was a struggle just to stay alive. How hard it must have been to have known a paradise and then to be told to leave it.

What must Eve have wanted the most at that moment?

What would *you* have wanted?

I believe that with all her heart Eve wished she could have taken back the instant just before she bit into the forbidden fruit—when her arm was still outstretched toward the limbs of the Tree of the Knowledge of Good and Evil and escape was still possible.

She ached to do things over, to have done things right the first time.

We are like Eve.

We have all experienced defeats and failures, trouble and turmoil.

We have all experienced a selfish heart, a shrewish spirit, anger, envy, and bitterness.

Some of our failures may not be so extreme as Eve's. They're not catastrophic, public events. Maybe they're just "small" lapses. But they still reveal how far our hearts are from where they ought to be. And we ache to do things over, to have lives of harmony and peace.

Whenever I lead a women's conference, I ask each of the women to fill out a prayer card, so our prayer team can intercede for them during the weekend. After the conference, I take the cards home and read through them myself. On more than one occasion, I have found myself weeping over those cards, my heart heavy for so many Christian women whose lives are in shambles.

Women whose marriages are hanging by a thread . . .

Women whose hearts ache for their children . . .

Women who are overwhelmed with past failures and wounds . . .

Women with intense personal struggles . . .

Women filled with doubts and confusion about their spiritual lives . . .

These women are real women. Their stories are real stories. Many of them have been in church all their lives. Some of them attend your church. One of them may be your child's Sunday school teacher. Some attend Bible study every week—they may even be Bible study leaders. In most cases, you'd never guess what's going on inside these women. When you ask how they are doing, they smile and say, "Fine."

These are the women whose stories have provided the impetus to write this book.

Please understand that these are not isolated testimonies. I am not talking about a few, extreme, "dysfunctional" women. I have read and heard enough such stories to fill this book.

Our culture is experiencing an epidemic of "soul-sickness"—not just among women "out there" in the world, but among those of us in the church.

In fact, if I had to describe a large percentage of the Christian women I have met and talked with in recent years, I would choose one or more of the following words:

frazzled	*defeated*
exhausted	*depressed*
burned-out	*ashamed*
overwhelmed	*emotionally unstable*
confused	*uptight*
angry	*insecure*
frustrated	*lonely*
discouraged	*fearful*
and, yes, even suicidal	

You would probably be amazed to learn how many people in any given audience of Christian women have contemplated taking their own lives—some of them within recent weeks or months. I have no doubt that someone who is reading this paragraph has come to the end of her rope. Maybe it's you. Maybe you feel it just isn't worth going on. Let me just say to you, dear one, "There *is* hope!" Reading this book won't make your problems go away, but I believe it will point you in the direction of Someone who can help. Please, please, keep reading.

Bondage is another word that comes to mind when I think of contemporary Christian women. The vast majority of women I meet are in bondage—they are not free, often, by their own admission. For example, many women live under a cloud of personal guilt and condemnation. They are not free to enjoy the grace and the love of God.

Many are in bondage to their past. Whether the result of their own failures or the failures of others, their pasts hang like huge weights around their necks—they carry them everywhere they go, trudging through life.

Others are in bondage to what the Bible calls the "fear of man"—they are gripped by fear of rejection, fear of what people think of them, and a longing for approval. Still others are emotional prisoners, enslaved by worry, fear, anger, depression, and self-pity.

One of the greatest areas of bondage women express is in relation to food—I have heard this from women of all sizes and shapes. Some can't stop eating; some can't make themselves eat. Both are in bondage.

I don't want to suggest that all women are "basket cases" (although we all have moments when we would describe ourselves that way!). But I am saying that, on the whole, Christian women are in trouble—deep trouble—the kind of trouble that requires more than superficial solutions and remedies.

When we turn to the Scriptures, we are reminded that God didn't intend for it to be this way. We read the words of Jesus in the gospel of John and know that God has something better for us:

> I am come that they might have life,
> and that they might have it more abundantly.

John 10:10 KJV

As you look at your life, would you say you are experiencing the abundant life Jesus came to give? Or do you find yourself just existing, coping, struggling, surviving?

I'm not asking if you have a trouble-free life. In fact, some of the most radiant, joyful women I know are women who are living in painfully difficult marriages; women who have wept at the graveside of a son or daughter; women who have been diagnosed with cancer or are caring for an elderly parent with Alzheimer's. But somehow, in the midst of the problems and the pain, they have discovered a source of life that enables them to walk through the valley with peace, confidence, and wholeness.

What about you? Do you relate to some of the women whose stories I shared above? Are there areas of bondage in your life?

What if I told you that instead of being miserable, frustrated, and in bondage, you could be

free	*confident*
joyous	*gracious*
contented	*peaceful*
loving	*stable*
radiant	

Do those words describe the kind of woman you would like to become?

Perhaps you are already experiencing the grace and peace of God in your life. Most likely, you know other women who are living in bondage, though they claim to have a relationship with Christ. Would you like to learn how to show them the pathway to freedom?

I'm not talking about a magic formula that will make problems vanish; I'm not offering any shortcuts to an easy life, nor am I promising the absence of pain and difficulties. Life is hard—there's no way around that. But I am talking about *walking through* the realities of life—things like rejection, loss, disappointment, wounds, and even death—in freedom and true joy.

You say, "That's what I want! I want it for myself; I want it for other women I know. Where do we begin?"

Through years of agonizing with women over their burdens and problems, and searching the Word of God for real answers, I have come to a simple but profound conclusion about the root of most of our struggles:

YOU AND I HAVE BEEN LIED TO.

WE HAVE BEEN DECEIVED.

In the pages that follow, I invite you to take a walk with me back to where all our problems began: the Garden of Eden, the first home of Adam and Eve—a perfect, ideal environment. What took place in that setting has an inescapable bearing on each of our lives as women today.

I want you to see how *a lie* was the starting place for all the trouble in the history of the universe. Eve had listened to that lie, believed that lie, and acted on that lie. Every problem, every war, every wound, every broken relationship, every heartache—it all goes back to *one simple lie.*

As lies have a way of doing, that first lie grew and spun off more lies. Eve believed the lie, and we, the daughters of Eve, have followed in her steps—listening to, believing, and acting on one lie after another. (Throughout this book, you will find fictionalized entries from "Eve's Diary." They are intended to suggest some of the lies Eve may have been vulnerable to at different seasons of her life. Her "diary" may even read a bit like yours, at points.)

The lies that have confronted women of all eras are beyond number. But certain lies seem to particularly plague Christian women in our day. My goal in this book is to expose those lies for what they really are. Some of the lies we will confront are so widely believed that you may find it difficult to recognize them as lies. But the "best" lies are those that look the most like the Truth. The "newest" lies are the oldest ones.

In addition to exposing some of the lies most commonly believed by Christian women, I want to rip the mask off the one who tells us those lies. Satan poses as an "angel of light" (2 Corinthians 11:14). He promises happiness and pretends to have our best interests at heart. But he is a deceiver and a destroyer; he is determined to dethrone God by getting us to side with him against God. I want you to see how Satan may have used some of the subtlest lies (or half-truths) to deceive and destroy you and those you love.

But we must do more than identify the Deceiver and his lies. I want to introduce you to the power of the Truth and to show you how believing and acting on the Truth is our means to freedom—not just survival, not escape—but true, glorious freedom, in the midst of this fallen, corrupt, hurting world.

Earlier this week, as I was out walking and meditating on several passages of Scripture, the Lord quickened to my heart the last two verses of the book of James:

My brothers, if one of you should wander from the truth and someone should bring him back, remember this: Whoever turns a sinner from the error of his way will save him from death and cover over a multitude of sins.

James 5:19–20

Immediately I sensed that in this passage the Lord was giving me the purpose and mission for writing this book. Millions of Christian women have been deceived and have wandered from the Truth. I have asked the Lord to use this book to help restore some of those women, to deliver them from bondage, and to set them free to walk in His grace, forgiveness, and abundant life.

Some of what I have to say will ruffle feathers. I have made no attempt to be "politically correct" or to merely write some nice thoughts that everyone will agree with. It is my belief that only radical surgery—that is, a radical adjustment of our way of thinking—will get to the root of our diseased hearts and make us whole. Sometimes the Truth hurts; it is rarely popular. But I would not be loving or kind if I failed to share with you the Truth that can set you free.

Two stories witness to the power of Truth.

I'm free! I had given up hope that it was possible, but God has set me completely free from years of bondage.

Those were the words of a young wife at an informal gathering as she began sharing with me what God has been doing in her life.

She told me how she had been in bondage to a particular moral habit ever since she was thirteen years old:

I tried and tried to stop; I did everything I knew to do—including Bible study, prayer, and being accountable to a friend—but I kept failing. When I blew it, I would confess my sin and ask God's forgiveness, but deep in my heart, I knew I would fall again. I just couldn't stop.

This woman has been a Christian for years; she and her husband have been active in Christian ministry; she has a genuine heart and hunger for the Lord and is involved in sharing her faith and ministering to others. But she had never been able to shake the enormous frustration and guilt within.

She became more animated as she described the process that led to the release she had longed to experience:

I finally got up the courage to ask a godly older woman for help. She encouraged me to ask God what lies I had been believing. I honestly didn't think I was believing any lies, but when I began to pray about it, God opened my eyes and showed me two major areas where I had been deceived. Those lies had kept me in bondage for over ten years! Once I saw the Truth, I repented of believing the lies and asked God to take back the ground I had allowed Satan to have in that area of my life.

Her countenance told the story of what happened next. "From that point," she said, "I have been totally free from this sin that had such a hold on my life. Plus, God is giving me victory in other areas where I have been tempted in the past. I can't begin to express to you the joy and freedom I have been experiencing. The Truth is so incredibly powerful!"

I witnessed the power of the Truth in another situation as I talked to a woman who had become emotionally involved with one of the pastors of her church. When I became aware of the situation, I called her at work because I did not know how much her husband knew. Since she was a receptionist for her company, I knew we might not have long to talk. After telling her who I was, I got right to the point, which I introduced with a word picture:

"If I looked out the window in the middle of the night and noticed that my neighbors' house was on fire, I would run next door and do whatever I had to do to get their attention and get them out of danger. If necessary, I would scream and pound on their door. I wouldn't worry about whether they felt annoyed because I was waking them up in the middle of the night. I wouldn't be the least concerned about hurting their feelings."

Then I said to this woman: "I have to tell you that you are in a burning house; you are in grave danger. Because this is a desperate situation, I'm not going to worry about what you think of me or about hurting your feelings. I'm going to do whatever I can to warn you about the danger you are in and to help you get out of that burning house before it's too late."

Tearfully, I begged this woman to realize the truth of what was happening in her life. I implored her to take immediate, drastic steps to extricate herself from the dangerous situation she had allowed herself to get into.

As we talked, God turned on the light in this woman's heart. I cannot take any credit for what happened in the days ahead—"For it is God who works in you to will and to act according to his good purpose" (Philippians 2:13). But what a joy it was to watch this dear lady embrace the Truth about her choices and about God's will for her life, marriage, and relationships. As she took one difficult step after another, the grace of God enabled her to move on, past her emotions, past old habits, past deeply ingrained (but false) ways of thinking. She began to walk in the Light. And in the Light she found a whole new way of life—the pathway of freedom and blessing.

That's how it is with Truth, and that is what I want for you, dear reader.

The journey you and I are about to take together may not be an easy one. It may be difficult—even painful—to identify and root out those areas of deception that have placed you in bondage. But I know a "Good Shepherd" who loves you dearly, who laid down His life for you, and who will take you by the hand and lead you into green pastures and by quiet waters, if only you will let Him.

It is for freedom that Christ has set us free.
Stand firm, then, and do not let yourselves
be burdened again by a yoke of slavery.

Galatians 5:1

"Come to me, all you who are weary and burdened,
and I will give you rest. Take my yoke upon you and learn
from me, for I am gentle and humble in heart,
and you will find rest for your souls.
For my yoke is easy and my burden is light."

Matthew 11:28–30

SECTION ONE

FOUNDATIONS

❧ PROLOGUE ☙

Dear diary,

My head is spinning. I hardly know where to start. This day started out so perfectly—like every other day we've ever had. As we always do, Adam and I got up early to take a walk with God. Those walks have always been the highlight of our day.

This morning, no one said anything for a while. We just enjoyed being together. Then God started singing. It was a love song. When He got to the chorus, we started to sing with Him—first, Adam's deep voice, then I joined in. We sang and sang and sang—songs about love and stars and joy and God. Finally, we all sat down under a big shade tree near the middle of the Garden. We thanked God for being so good; we told Him all we wanted to do was to make Him happy and to find our happiness in Him. It was such a sweet time—it always was when the three of us were together.

I don't know how to explain what happened next. All of a sudden, we heard a voice we'd never heard before. I turned and there, looking right at me, was the most beautiful creature I had ever seen. He talked directly to me. He made me feel important, and I found myself wanting to hear what he had to say.

I'm not sure what happened to God at this point. It wasn't like He left us. I think I just kind of forgot He was there. In fact, for a while, I forgot Adam was there. I felt as if I were alone with this dazzling, mysterious creature.

The conversation that followed is indelibly etched in my mind. He asked me questions—questions I'd never thought about before. Then he offered me some things I had never had before—things I'd never thought I needed. Independence—from God and from Adam. Position—I had always looked up to God and Adam; this creature said they would look up to me. Knowledge—of mysteries known only to God. Permission—to eat the fruit from the tree in the middle of the Garden.

First, I just listened and looked. In my heart, I pondered, I questioned, I debated. Adam had reminded me many times that God had said we must not eat the fruit from that tree. The creature kept looking into my eyes and talking in that soothing voice. I found myself believing him. It felt so right. Finally, I surrendered. I reached out—cautiously at first, then more boldly. I took. I ate. I handed it to Adam. He ate. We ate together—first me, then him.

Those next moments are a blur. Sensations deep down inside that I've never had before. New awareness—like I know a secret I'm not supposed to know. Elation and depression—at the same time. Liberation. Prison. Rising. Falling. Confident. Afraid. Ashamed. Dirty. Hiding—I can't let Him see me like this.

Alone. So very alone. Lost. Deceived.

CHAPTER ONE

TRUTH...OR CONSEQUENCES

"Become a World-Class Violinist Instantaneously."

"How to Play the Piano...Instantly!"

"'Instant Health' at the Flip of a Switch!" (Ad for a kitchen appliance)

"Melt 10 lbs. in 10 minutes!...a workout so easy, you do it in your pajamas!"

"Delivers so much peace of mind it should be covered under your health plan." (Ad for a popular car)

"Look Better and Feel Younger in Just Minutes a Day...The key to a healthier, happier life." (Ad for an oxygen chamber. Price tag: $3,999.95)

Our culture is riddled with deception. It is everywhere, as illustrated by these kinds of outlandish advertising claims. Sometimes it is easy to see through the falsehood (as in the claim that one can become a world-class violinist instantaneously). Unfortunately, however, most deception is not quite so easy to detect.

Deception in advertising appeals to our natural human longings. We *want* to believe that somehow, mysteriously, those unwanted pounds really could melt away in just ten minutes—no sweat, no discipline, no cost, no effort, no pain. That's why we buy the pills, the diet drink powders, and the exercise equipment sold on infomercials.

A clever and cunning pitchman whose intention was to change Adam and Eve's thinking about God and His ways designed the first advertising campaign. Satan's objective was to drive a wedge between God and His creatures. He rightly assumed that the man and woman were not likely to support anything that appeared to be an all-out assault on God. He knew that, instead, he would have to subtly trick them, to deceive them, to seduce them by making an offer that appeared to be reasonable, desirable, and not entirely "anti-God."

Satan deceived Eve through a clever combination of outright lies, half-truths, and falsehoods disguised as truth. He began by planting seeds of doubt in her mind about what God had actually said ("Did God really say . . . ?" [Genesis 3:1]).

Next he led her to be careless with the word of God and to suggest that God had said something that, in fact, He had not said. God had said, "Do not *eat* the fruit of the tree." However, Eve quoted God as saying, "You must not *touch* it" (v. 3, italics added).

Satan deceived Eve by causing her to question the goodness, love, and motives of God. "Did God really say, 'You must not eat from any tree in the garden'?" he asked. The implication was: "Has God put restrictions on your freedom? Sounds like He doesn't want you to be happy."

The Truth is that God had said, "'You are *free* to eat from any tree in the garden' [2:16, italics added]—except one."

The Truth is that God is a generous God.

In that entire, vast Garden, God had posted only one Keep Off sign: "Do not eat from the Tree of the Knowledge of Good and Evil." Furthermore, the one restriction God imposed was in the best interests of the couple and was intended to guarantee their long-term blessing and happiness. God knew that when they ate of that tree, they would die; their relationship with Him would be severed; they would become slaves—to Satan, sin, and self.

The Serpent further deceived Eve by lying to her about the consequences of choosing to disobey God. God had said, "When you eat of it you will surely die" (2:17). Satan countered: "You will *not* surely die" (3:4, italics added). He flatly contradicted what God had already said.

The devil seduced Eve by offering her all kinds of benefits if she would just eat the forbidden fruit (3:5). He promised that a whole world of knowledge and experience would open up to her ("Your eyes will be opened"). He assured her that she would be equal with God—that is, that she could be her own god ("You will be like God").

Finally, he promised that she would be able to decide for herself what was right and wrong ("knowing good and evil"). God had already told Adam and Eve what was right and what was wrong. But Satan said, in essence, "That's His opinion; you're entitled to your own opinion—you can make your own decisions about what is right and wrong."

Satan deceived Eve by causing her to make her decision based on what she could see and on what her emotions and her reason told her to be right, even when it was contrary to what God had already told the couple:

When the woman saw that the fruit of the tree was good for food and pleasing to the eye, and also desirable for gaining wisdom, she took some and ate it.

Genesis 3:6

Eve took the bite. But instead of the promised rewards, she found herself with a mouth full of worms—shame, guilt, fear, and alienation. She had been lied to—she had been deceived.

As Puritan pastor Thomas Brooks put it,

> Satan promises the best, but pays with the worst; he promises honor, and pays with disgrace; he promises pleasure, and pays with pain; he promises profit, and pays with loss; he promises life, and pays with death.[1]

From that moment to this, Satan has used deception to win our affections, influence our choices, and destroy our lives. In one way or another, every problem we have in this world is the fruit of deception—the result of believing something that simply isn't true.

Satan holds out the glittering promise of "real life"; he knows, however, that those who respond to his offer will certainly die (Proverbs 14:12).

So why do we fall for his deception? Why do we go for the lure? One reason is that Satan doesn't usually appear in the form of a serpent—instead, he comes disguised as a *New York Times* best-seller, a popular magazine, or a movie, or a TV show, or a Top Ten hit song. He may also pose as a relative or friend giving sincere counsel, a therapist, or even a Christian writer, preacher, or counselor.

Regardless of the immediate source, anytime we receive input that is not consistent with the Word of God we can be sure Satan is trying to deceive and destroy us. What we read or hear may sound right, may feel right, may seem right—but if it is contrary to the Word of God, it *isn't* right. If we could only see that the forbidden fruit, fruit that looks so ripe and tastes so sweet in the first moment, always leads ultimately to death and destruction.

THE STRATEGY OF DECEPTION

Deception was—and still is—crucial to Satan's strategy. According to Jesus, it is the devil's very nature to deceive:

[The devil] was a murderer from the beginning,
not holding to the truth, for there is no truth in him.
When he lies, he speaks his native language,
for he is a liar and the father of lies.

John 8:44

For reasons we cannot fully understand, Satan chose to target the woman for his strategy of deception. Twice in the New Testament the apostle Paul points out that it was the woman who was deceived: "The serpent beguiled Eve through his subtilty" (2 Corinthians 11:3 KJV); "Adam was not the one deceived; it was the woman who was deceived" (1 Timothy 2:14).

Some theologians believe there was something in the way Eve was created that made her more vulnerable to deception—that she was inherently more "temptable," or "seducible." Others suggest that because God had placed her under the headship of her husband, once she stepped out from under that spiritual covering and protection, she was more easily deceived.

Regardless, the point is that as fallen women, we are particularly prone to fall prey to Satan's deception. Remember that he did not first approach the man; he deliberately approached and deceived the woman. It was the woman who led her husband into sin, and together they led the whole human race into sin (though Adam, as head, is held ultimately responsible). I believe there is something significant about that progression and that, to this day, there is a unique sense in which Satan targets women for deception. This is part of his strategy. He knows that if we as women buy into his deception, we will influence the men around us to sin, and our sinful choices will set a pattern for subsequent generations to follow.

Sometimes, as was the case with Eve, Satan deceives us directly. Sometimes, however, he uses other people as instruments of deception.

In the fifth chapter of Ephesians, Paul warns, "Let no one deceive you with empty words" (v. 6). Repeatedly, he challenges God's people to speak Truth to one another. When we are not honest with each other, we actually do Satan's work for him, acting as his agents, deceiving and destroying each other.

According to the Scripture, we can even be deceived by spiritual leaders—those who have been entrusted with the responsibility of shepherding God's flock and communicating the Truth to His people. Sadly, many leaders abuse their calling and their followers by failing to speak the Truth. Through the prophet Ezekiel, God addresses those leaders who deceive people:

> With lies ye have made the heart of the righteous sad . . . ;
> and strengthened the hands of the wicked,
> that he should not return from his wicked way,
> by promising him life.
>
> *Ezekiel 13:22 KJV*

I believe this is an accurate description of much of what is taking place in the Christian world today. Walk into almost any Christian bookstore, leaf through many Christian periodicals, tune in to many religious radio and television broadcasts, listen to many popular Christian mental health professionals, and you will find respected "Christian leaders" who are deceiving their followers. In most cases, I do not believe they intend to deceive people—in fact, they may not even realize they are being deceptive. However, that is exactly what is happening.

In many cases, they "strengthen the hands of the wicked" by suggesting they do not need to repent. They promise God's blessing and grace to people who do not qualify because of their willful disobedience and unrepentant hearts. Their teachings help people justify . . .

- anger ("healthy expression of your true feelings");
- selfishness ("You've got to place boundaries between you and demanding people");
- irresponsibility ("You are dysfunctional because you have been deeply wounded by others"); and
- infidelity ("You are free to divorce your mate and marry someone else; God is the God of the second chance").

At the same time, they make "the righteous" feel "sad" or guilty . . .

34

- for taking personal responsibility ("You're codependent");
- for demonstrating a servant's heart ("You shouldn't let others take advantage of you"); and
- for being faithful to their vows ("God does not expect you to stay in that marriage").

OPEN YOUR EYES

Sadly, most people—even Christians—have unthinkingly exposed themselves to so much deception that they do not even realize they are being deceived. That is the very nature of deception—it blinds us to the fact that we have been deceived.

One of my goals in this book is to urge Christian women to open their eyes and begin to evaluate what is going on around them—to wake up to the deception that is so pervasive in both our secular and our Christian cultures. So much of our lifestyle is rooted in ways of thinking that simply are not true. The result is a house built on sinking sand. One lie leads to another and another and another.

Unfortunately, most people mindlessly accept whatever they hear and see. We listen to music, read books and magazines, watch movies, listen to advice, and respond to advertisements without asking ourselves important questions:

- "What is the message here?"
- "Is it really true?"
- "Am I being deceived by a way of thinking that is contrary to the Truth?"

Satan's promise to Eve was tantalizing: "Your eyes will be opened, and you will be like God, knowing good and evil" (Genesis 3:5). Who could resist such an extraordinary offer?

The forbidden fruit was "*good* for food and *pleasing* to the eye, and also *desirable* for gaining wisdom" (v. 6, italics added). If it hadn't seemed so attractive, do you think Eve would have fallen for the offer? If that fruit had been rotten and crawling with worms, would she have considered disobeying God? Of course not. What makes Satan's offers so alluring and so deceptive is that they look so right.

The problem is that Eve didn't stop to evaluate what was really happening. She didn't take time to discern truth from error. She didn't stop to consider the cost and the consequences of what she was about to do. If Eve could have imagined the ugly, painful, deadly consequences of her choice—in her own life, in her relationship with God, in her marriage, in her children, in her children's children, and (through the sin of her husband, who followed her) in every human being that would ever live on the planet—do you think she would have listened to Satan's lie and disobeyed God? I doubt it.

But we have precisely the same problem. I have discovered that very few Christians seriously consider the consequences of their choices. We simply live our lives, responding to the people, circumstances, and influences around us—eating what we crave at the moment, buying the newest gadget advertised on TV, adopting the latest fads, and embracing the lifestyles, values, and priorities of our friends. It all looks so good; it feels so right; it seems so innocent. But we end up in abusive relationships, head over heels in debt, angry, frustrated, trapped, and overwhelmed. We have been deceived. We have fallen for a lie.

In an unforgettable example of this kind of deception, a young mother of seven children told me that she had become involved with a man she had met on the Internet; she was thinking of leaving her husband for this other man. As we met together one night, she acknowledged that what she was doing was wrong. "But," she said, "he is so good to me and to my children."

For two hours, I begged her to see that this man was not truly interested in her or her children—if he were, he would not be breaking up her marriage; if he really loved her, he would not be leading her to violate God's law. I warned her that the road she was on, though it seemed so appealing, would certainly lead to destruction. I tried to help her see that she had been deceived and that her only hope was to believe and embrace the Truth.

THE PROGRESSION FROM
DECEPTION TO BONDAGE

In the chapters that follow, we will examine some of the most common and destructive lies women believe; but first, let's take a look at how we become deceived and how deception leads to bondage.

Generally speaking, people don't fall into bondage overnight. They don't just wake up one morning and discover that they are addicted to food or have a temper they can't control. There is a progression that leads to bondage, and it always begins when we . . .

LISTEN TO A LIE.

That's how it all began in the Garden of Eden. Eve *listened* to the lies told her by Satan. I am confident she had no idea where those lies would ultimately lead her and her family. Perhaps it didn't seem particularly dangerous just to *listen* to the Serpent—to hear him out, to see what he had to say. Listening in itself wasn't disobedience. But—and here's the key—listening to a viewpoint that was contrary to God's word put Eve on a slippery slope that led to disobedience, which led to physical and spiritual death.

Listening to things that are not true is the first step toward ultimate bondage and death. That is why I believe it is so important to carefully monitor the input we allow into our minds and hearts.

I am the oldest of seven children, and I thank the Lord for the conviction God gave my parents about controlling the kinds of influence that were allowed in our home as we were growing up.

My parents were first-generation Christians—they did not come to know the Lord until they were young adults. When they were raising our family, they did not have the advantage of many of the wonderful resources and seminars that are available to parents today. However, God gave them the wisdom and courage to "grow" their children in a spiritual "greenhouse." They made a conscious effort to protect us from influences that could be harmful and to surround us with influences that would spiritually nurture our lives. As a result, we grew up with well-protected hearts. At a young age, our hearts were sensitized to sin and we learned to discern between right and wrong.

This approach to child rearing did not always make sense to us when we were kids. But how I thank the Lord today that my parents had the courage to say, "We are not going to knowingly allow our children to be influenced by the lies promoted in this world." They earnestly desired that we would grow up to love the Word and the ways of God, that our hearts would be quickened by the Truth, and that we would embrace it for ourselves. Once they released us from that greenhouse environment into the world, they wanted us to continue to walk in the Truth and to recognize and reject anything that was deceptive and untrue.

As an adult, I still find it is crucial to guard my mind—to carefully choose the input I allow into my life and to reject that which promotes ungodly thinking. The world's deceptive way of thinking comes to us through so many avenues—television, magazines, movies, music, friends, malls, and catalogs, to name a few. A steady diet of these worldly influences will shape our view of what is valuable, what is beautiful, and what is important in life.

There are no harmless lies. We cannot expose ourselves to the world's false, deceptive way of thinking and come out unscathed. Eve's first mistake was not eating the fruit; her first mistake was listening to the Serpent.

Listening to counsel or ways of thinking that are not according to the Truth is the first step in developing wrong beliefs that will ultimately place us in bondage. Once we have listened to the lie, the next step toward bondage is that we . . .

DWELL ON THE LIE.

First we listen to it; then we dwell on it. We begin to consider what the Enemy has said. We mull it over in our minds. We engage the Enemy in conversation. We contemplate that he may be right, after all. The process can be likened to farming or gardening. First, the soil is cultivated—we open ourselves up to input that is contrary to God's Word. Then, the seed is sown—we listen to the lie. Next, the seed is watered and fertilized—we dwell on the lie.

If we allow our minds and hearts to dwell on things that are not true, sooner or later, we will . . .

BELIEVE THE LIE.

At this point, the seed that has been sown begins to take root and starts to grow. First Eve listened to the Serpent's sales pitch. Then she considered it and engaged him in further discussion about it. Before long, she believed that what he told her was true—in spite of the fact that it clearly contradicted the Truth of what God had already said. Once she believed the lie, the next step was a small one. Listen to the lie, dwell on it, believe it, and sooner or later you will . . .

ACT ON THE LIE.

Now the seed that has been sown, watered, and fertilized and has taken root begins to produce fruit—the fruit of deception. Beliefs produce behavior. Believing things that aren't true produces sinful behavior. What we believe will be seen in the way we live. Conversely, the way we behave is invariably based on what we believe to be true—not what we *say* we believe, but what we *actually* believe. "As [a man] *thinketh* in his heart, so *is* he" (Proverbs 23:7 KJV, italics added).

The important thing to remember is that *every act of sin in our lives begins with a lie.* We listen to the lie; we dwell on it until we believe it; finally, we act on it.

Now watch what happens next. We reject the Truth and violate the Word of God one time in what seems to be just "a little matter." However, the next time we are tempted, we find that it is easier to sin; the next time, it is easier still. We don't just sin once; we sin again and again and again, until a "groove" has been worn in our hearts—a sinful pattern. Before we realize what has happened, we are in bondage. A sinful stronghold has been established. Satan threw out the bait, we took it, and now he has reeled us in and made us his catch.

Don't miss how the progression got started:

EVERY AREA OF BONDAGE IN OUR LIVES CAN BE TRACED BACK TO A LIE.

A seed is sown; it is watered and fertilized; it takes root and produces fruit—not just a single piece of fruit, but a whole harvest—a harvest of bondage, destruction, and death.

MOVING FROM BONDAGE TO FREEDOM

Most of us have areas of our lives where we are in bondage because we have listened to, believed, and acted on lies. How can we escape from bondage and begin to move toward freedom in those practical issues of our lives? Here are three steps to keep in mind as we begin to deal more specifically with the lies that put us in bondage and the Truth that sets us free.

1. *Identify the area(s) of bondage or sinful behavior.* Chances are, you already know what some of those bondages are. But there may be others that are not as obvious. Ask God to show you specific areas

where you are not free. The Scripture says, "A man is a slave to whatever has mastered him" (2 Peter 2:19). What are the issues in your life where you are not living in freedom as a child of God?

Are there areas where you are in physical bondage (overeating, an eating disorder, substance abuse)? Are you in emotional bondage (anxiety, fear, depression, chronic emotional disorders), sexual bondage (masturbation, pornography, lust, fornication, homosexuality), or financial bondage (overspending, greed, stinginess)? Are there sinful habits that plague you (anger, lying)? Are you in bondage to the need for approval, excessive shyness, talking too much, or an addiction to TV or romance novels? God may bring other areas of bondage to your mind.

Once you identify those areas, don't just try to eliminate them. In fact, you may have already tried to deal with these behaviors, failed, and been tempted to give up. If you want to get rid of poisonous berries growing on your property, it's not enough to go out and pick all the berries off the bush. More will just grow back in their place. The only way to permanently get rid of the poisonous fruit is to pull the bush out from the roots. That's why this next step is so important.

2. *Identify the lie(s) at the root of that bondage or behavior.* What lies have you listened to, believed, and acted on that have put you in bondage? The answer to that question may not be immediately apparent—roots are generally hidden beneath the surface, and lies, by their very nature, are deceptive. We need the Lord to help us see what we have been believing that is not true.

In the pages that follow, we will identify forty lies that many Christian women have allowed to take root and produce fruit in their lives. Ask God to show you which of the Enemy's lies you have bought into—whether the ones in this book or others He brings to mind—and to help you repent of believing those lies. Once you identify the specific lies you have believed, what next?

3. *Replace the lie(s) with the Truth.* Satan is a powerful enemy. His primary weapon is deception. His lies are powerful. But there is

something even more powerful than Satan's lies—and that is the Truth. Once we identify the lies that have put us in bondage and repent of believing those lies, we have an effective weapon to overcome deception—the weapon of Truth.

Each lie must be countered with the corresponding Truth. Where we have listened to, dwelt on, believed, and acted on lies, we must begin to listen to, meditate on, believe, and act on the Truth. That is how we will move from bondage to freedom, by the power of the Spirit of God. As Jesus declared, it is the Truth that "will set you free" (John 8:32).

LIES WOMEN BELIEVE

CHAPTER TWO

LIES WOMEN BELIEVE... ABOUT GOD

Dear diary,

I am so confused. Yesterday morning, I was so sure about a lot of things. Now I don't know who—or what—to believe. I've never had reason to doubt that God loved me. I had a thousand reasons to believe He was good. I never wondered if He was telling us the truth. I trusted Him. I believed what He said.

Now, for some reason, He doesn't seem like the same God who walked and talked and sang with us every morning. If He is so good, why didn't He stop me from talking to the Serpent or eating the fruit? Why did He make the fruit look so good? Why did He put that tree there, anyway? And why did He care if we ate that fruit?

He seems so far away. I'm afraid of Him. He said we would die if we ate from that tree. That seems like an awfully harsh punishment—hardly seems fair—especially for a first offense. Today

He told us we have to leave Eden. Why couldn't He have given us
a second chance? Does He really care what happens to us?
This whole thing is such a mess. Can't God do something?

As we begin to identify some of the lies women believe, let me
assure you that this is by no means an exhaustive list. Satan is a master Deceiver, and his lies are endless. My goal is simply to address some
of the lies that are most commonly believed by "church women"
today. I believe these particular lies are at the root of much of the
bondage that exists among Christian women. (Throughout the rest
of the book, I have interspersed testimonies I have received from
women who share the consequences they have experienced as a result of believing these lies.)

Of course, no woman believes all the lies. You will probably find
that you are tempted to believe certain lies (or variations on them).
Satan knows where you are most vulnerable to being deceived, and
that is where he will target his attack.

Your first response to some of these lies may be, "I don't believe
that." One of Satan's strategies is to blind us to the lies we have bought
into—to make us assume that because we *know* the Truth, we also
believe the Truth. Countless times over the years, I have counseled with
women who claim to believe the Truth of God's Word; but the way
they live—their choices, their priorities, their response to pain—reveals that they do not really believe the Truth. However, what we believe is revealed, not by what we know or what we *say* we believe, but
by how we actually *live*. So as we walk through these lies, it's not
enough to ask, "Do I believe this lie?" Each of us must also ask, "Do
I *live* as though I believe this lie?"

A number of these lies are particularly deceptive because they
are half-truths, rather than outright lies. That makes them even more
subtle and dangerous. The fact is, a half-truth will put you in bondage
just as surely as a whole lie.

We will not take time to develop each lie as fully as it deserves
to be treated. Entire books have been written on many of these subjects. My goal is not to present a comprehensive explanation of what

in some cases are major issues but, rather, to give a broad overview of the kind of thinking that I believe has wreaked havoc in the lives and homes of Christian women.

On page 269, you will find a list of resources related to key topics addressed in this book. I would encourage you to refer to that section for further assistance with issues of particular concern to you, especially if you find yourself in an extreme or severe situation that is beyond the scope of this book.

Some of the issues we will address are "hot potatoes." They are controversial, even in the evangelical world. In a few cases, you may find yourself saying, "I don't believe that is a lie."

Let me appeal to you not to get tripped up by a handful of particular issues where you may have a genuine disagreement. I am simply presenting what I understand the Scripture to teach. I am not the final word on any of these matters; Jesus and His Word are "the Truth." My objective is not for you to agree with everything I say but to motivate you to seek out the Truth as it is revealed in the Word of God and to examine and evaluate every area of your life in light of that Truth.

I have chosen to start by dealing with lies that women believe about God because there is nothing more crucial than what we believe about God. As Hannah Whitall Smith points out in her spiritual autobiography, *The Unselfishness of God,*

> Everything in your spiritual life depends on the sort of God you worship. Because the character of the worshiper will always be molded by the character of what he worships: If it is a cruel and revengeful God, the worshiper will be the same, but if it is a loving, tender, forgiving, unselfish God, the worshiper will be transformed slowly, wonderfully, into this likeness.[1]

What we believe about God is foundational to our whole belief system. If we have wrong thinking about God, we will have wrong thinking about everything else. What we believe about God determines the way we live. If we believe things about Him that aren't true, we will eventually act on those lies and end up in bondage.

1. "GOD IS NOT REALLY GOOD. IF HE WERE, HE WOULD..."

This is a lie that few women consciously believe. Most of us would never *say*, "God is not really good." We know better. Theologically, intellectually, we know that God is good. But deep in many of our hearts, there lurks a suspicion that He may not really be good—at least, that He has not been good *to me*.

I believe this lie is at the core of much of our wrong thinking about God. In essence, this is the lie Satan used to seduce Eve back in the Garden. God had blessed the man and woman and created a whole paradise for their enjoyment. He had given them the freedom to partake of the fruit on every tree—except one.

If you have any doubt about the goodness of God, go back and reread the first two chapters of Genesis. There you see a personal, generous, good God. Everything He made was good—because it was a reflection of His goodness.

When Satan wanted to tempt the woman to rebel against God, he did so by planting in her mind a seed of doubt about God's goodness: "Did God really say, 'You must not eat from any tree in the garden'?" (Genesis 3:1). The implication was that "God must not be good—if He were, He would not have denied you something you really wanted."

When turbulence, disappointment, or pain comes into our lives; when we lose people we love; when things don't go as we had hoped or planned, Satan tempts us to wonder, "Is God really good? If He were, how could He have let this happen?" or "Why would He have kept this [good thing] from me?" In this fallen world where wars, genocide, famine, and natural disasters are a reality, the Deceiver tries to cast God in a negative light: "How could a truly good God let the Holocaust take place? Or the famine in Ethiopia? Or the massacre at Columbine?"

Once we doubt the goodness of God, we feel justified in rejecting His will and making our own decisions about right and wrong.

The Truth is, God *is* good. Whether or not His choices seem good to us, He is good. Whether or not we feel it, He is good. Whether or not it seems true in my life or yours, He is still good.

I will never forget the day I first consciously found refuge in this Truth. I had spent the weekend of my twenty-first birthday at home, visiting my parents and six brothers and sisters. On Saturday afternoon, my parents took me to the airport to catch a flight to Virginia, where I was serving on the staff of a local church.

When I landed in Lynchburg, I received a call from my mother telling me that my father had had a heart attack and had instantly gone to be with the Lord. There was no warning. No time to say final goodbyes. My forty-year-old mother was left with seven children, ages eight to twenty-one.

Over the next few days, and in the weeks and months that followed, the tears flowed freely. Each of us had shared a close relationship with this extraordinary husband and father. Everyone who knew Art DeMoss felt an enormous sense of loss when he was taken to heaven.

But in that moment when I first learned of my dad's homegoing, the Lord did something especially gracious for me—He reminded me of the Truth. Before there was any other conscious thought, before there were any tears, He brought to mind a verse I had read not many days earlier. Paraphrased, the verse read: "God is good, and everything He does is good" (Psalm 119:68).

My dad had spent the first twenty-one years of my life teaching me that Truth. Now, at that crucial moment, the Truth proved to be a fortress for my heart. I missed my dad terribly—I still do at times, more than twenty years later. I never knew him in my adult life. There are so many things I wish we could talk about. But I knew then, and I know now, that God is good and everything He does is good. Hannah Whitall Smith put it well when she said,

> A great many things in God's divine providences do not look to the eye like goodness. But faith sits down before mysteries such as these, and says, "The Lord is good, therefore all that He does must be good no matter how it looks. I can wait for His explanations."[2]

☙ 2. "GOD DOESN'T LOVE ME."

This lie is often related to the previous one. Again, few of us would actually admit to believing this because, in our minds, we know we are supposed to believe that God does love us. But for many women, there is a disconnection between what they know intellectually and what they *feel* to be true. And therein lies one of our problems: We trust what we *feel* to be true, rather than what we *know* to be true. (We will come back to this point because it is so fundamental to the way we as women are wired.)

We look around at our relationships—a loveless marriage; rejection by an ex-mate; grown children who won't call home or come to visit; approaching forty, and not a suitor in sight—and our feelings tell us: "Nobody loves me—not even God. He may love the world, He may love everyone else, but He doesn't really love me. If He did, I wouldn't feel so lonely and unloved." We'd never say this aloud—but that is what we *feel* to be true. So the seed of a lie is planted in our minds; we dwell on the lie until we believe it to be true; sooner or later, our behavior reflects what we really believe; and we end up in bondage.

Perhaps you can relate to "Victoria's" background.

❧ ❧

I come from a somewhat difficult and distant family, in which love was always conditional. As a result, it was very hard for me to believe God could really love me unconditionally. That brought undue condemnation whenever I would make a mistake and sin—not that sin is anything to be overlooked—but I did not believe God would forgive me.

❧ ❧

It is no small matter to give in to the lie that "God doesn't love me." The implications are enormous and affect every other area of our lives and relationships. Tiny little seeds, allowed to take root in our minds, grow up to produce a great big harvest.

The Truth is, God *does* love us. Whether or not we feel loved, regardless of what we have done or where we have come from, He loves us with an infinite, incomprehensible love.

God loves me—not because I have loved Him since I was four years old, not because I seek to please Him, not because I speak at conferences and write books. He loves me—because He *is* love. His love for me is not based on anything I have ever done or ever could do for Him. It is not based on my performance. I do not deserve His love and could never earn it.

The Scripture says that when I was His enemy, *He loved me.* You say, "How could you have been God's enemy when you were a little girl?" According to the Bible, from the moment I was born, I was ungodly, a sinner, God's enemy, and deserving of His eternal wrath (Romans 5:6–10). In spite of my alienation from Him, He loved me and sent His Son to die for me. He loved me in eternity past; He will love me for all of eternity future. There is nothing I could do to make Him love me any less; there is nothing I could do to make Him love me any more.

Melana Monroe is a friend who has faced a long, hard battle with breast cancer. In a recent letter, she talked about how she has come to have a deeper comprehension of the incredible love of God, through her husband's response to her double mastectomy:

As we wept and trembled when he took my bandages off the first time, I was so ugly, scarred, and bald. I was in intense grief that I could never be a whole wife to him again. Steve held me tightly and with tears in his eyes said, "Melana, I love you because that is who I am."

I instantly recognized Christ in my husband. As His bride, we are also eaten up with cancer—sin—and are scarred, mutilated, and ugly, but He loves us because that is who He is. No comeliness in us draws Christ's attention; it is only His essence that draws Him to us.

Hannah Whitall Smith invites us to contemplate the vastness, the height, the depth, the greatness of the love of God:

Put together all the tenderest love you know of, the deepest you have ever felt, and the strongest that has ever been poured out upon you, and heap upon it all the love of all the loving human hearts in the world, and then multiply it by infinity, and you will begin, perhaps, to have some faint glimpse of what the love of God is.[3]

3. "GOD IS JUST LIKE MY FATHER."

As women, our view of God is often greatly influenced by the men we have known—particularly our fathers. Our perception of God can be positively or negatively shaped by those men. I am blessed and deeply grateful to have had a loving, faithful, involved father. This has made it easier for me to trust my heavenly Father and to receive His love.

However, many women have had just the opposite experience. Your father may have been distant, absent, overbearing, harsh, abusive, or unable to express love. If so, the idea of God's being your "Father" may make you cringe. You may relate to these women:

I had a stepfather who was cruel to me, and it is very hard to accept that God is not like him.

My dad is a Christian and a good guy, but I have never heard much encouragement from him. For instance, when I would help him paint, I would say, "Does this look okay?" hoping to hear, "Hey, that looks really nice!" But he would only say, "Try not to _____ [whatever]." Maybe that is why I imagined God's finding fault instead of loving me unconditionally and accepting me.

If you have been wounded by a father—or another man you trusted—you may find it difficult to trust God. You may even be afraid of Him or angry with Him. You must believe me when I tell you that God is not like any man you have ever known. The wisest, kindest earthly father is but a pale reflection of our heavenly Father. The God of the Bible is infinitely more wonderful and pure and loving than even the most wonderful father. That is why it is so important that we not allow our view of God to be determined by other men, for at their very best they are flawed representations of God.

If you want to know what God is really like, you need to turn to the Word of God, which clearly reveals what He is like; you need to get to know Jesus, who is the "radiance of God's glory and the exact representation of his being" (Hebrews 1:3).

The God of the Bible is a compassionate, tender, merciful Father. That doesn't mean He gives us everything we want—no wise father would give his children everything they want. It doesn't mean we can always understand His decisions—He is far too great for that. It doesn't mean He never allows us to suffer pain—in fact, at times, He actually inflicts pain and hardship upon us. Why? Because He loves us. Because He cares about us. Because He is committed to us. Hebrews tells us, "God disciplines us for our good, that we may share in his holiness" (12:10).

Regardless of how we feel or what we think, the fact remains that He is a good Father who dearly loves His children—a Father who can be trusted with our lives. Hannah Whitall Smith's writings have much to say about the implications of knowing and trusting the Father heart of God:

> Discomfort and unrest are impossible to souls who come to know that God is their Father.
>
> ...What a good earthly father would not do, God who is our Father would not do either; and what a good father ought to do, God who is our Father is absolutely sure to do.
>
> Christ has declared to us the name of the Father in order that we may discover that the Father loves us as He loves His Son. If we believed this,

could we ever have an anxious or rebellious thought again? Would we not believe in every conceivable circumstance that the divine Father would care for us in the best possible way and meet our every need?[4]

4. "GOD IS NOT REALLY ENOUGH."

"Christ is all I need, all that I need." It's one thing to sing that little chorus when we're sitting in a church service. But when we walk out the church doors and into the rough–and–tumble world, do we really believe He is *all* we need? As with the first three lies, we would hardly dare to breathe these words; few of us consciously believe this lie. But the way we live reveals that this is what we really do believe.

When it comes down to it, we don't believe God's Word is truly sufficient to deal with our problems. Oh, it can deal with everyone else's problems; but it doesn't speak to *my* issues, *my* needs, *my* relationships, *my* situation. I need God's Word *plus* these eight books from the Christian bookstore; I need God's Word *plus* tapes and conferences and counselors.

Sure, I need God. But I need Him *plus* close friends; I need Him *plus* good health; I need Him *plus* a husband; I need Him *plus* children; I need Him *plus* a job that pays enough; I need Him *plus* a house with a microwave, a washer/dryer, a garage, and a fresh paint job . . .

Do you really believe that if you have God you have enough? Or are you more like these women:

"God is not really enough"—I did not know I believed this until I realized how much trust I put in other things and people. I thought I trusted God fully and kept telling my husband we just needed to trust God, but then I would run to my friends to discuss our marriage or finances.

I have turned to food for comfort when things were going bad in our marriage. In forty years of marriage, I have put on forty-five extra pounds.

I have denied the truth that my relationship with Jesus will satisfy my longings. Through the way I live, I have shown those around me that I need "things" in order to be happy. I have been critical, complaining, and irritable most of my life. I have been living this lie.

Do we truly believe God is enough, or are we looking to other things and people to fill the empty places of our hearts—food, shopping, friends, hobbies, vacations, our job, or our family?

5. "GOD'S WAYS ARE TOO RESTRICTIVE."

Over and over again, the Scripture teaches that God's laws are for our good and our protection. Obedience is the pathway to freedom. But Satan places in our minds the idea that God's laws are burdensome, unreasonable, and unfair, and that if we obey Him we will be miserable. In the Garden, he caused Eve to focus on the one limitation God had placed on her. The Deceiver's motto is "Have it your way: no one has the right to tell you what you can or cannot do."

If we're honest, many of us can identify with "Sarah":

I felt that putting restrictions on my behavior was depriving me of pleasure and of what was good. I ate whatever I wanted, whenever I wanted it, and in whatever quantities I wanted because I felt punished by saying no.

I have often wondered why food is such an issue with so many women. I'm convinced it has something to do with Genesis 3. After all, what was the very first sin? It was the sin of *overeating*. The single restriction God put on her diet was one too many for Eve. Like "Sarah," she felt that "putting restrictions on her behavior was depriving her of pleasure and of what was good." So what did she do? (Remember—beliefs determine behavior.) She "ate whatever she wanted."

So we throw off the restrictions, determined to "have it our way." We are free to choose our own way, just as Eve was free to eat the forbidden fruit. But there is one thing we are not free to choose, and that is the consequences.

We have said that believing and acting on a lie will ultimately lead to bondage. Listen to the rest of "Sarah's" testimony:

When I understood that true freedom comes from obedience, I was freed from bondage to food—I lost sixty-five pounds, as well as the depression I had experienced.

"Sarah" had decided to eat what she wanted, whenever she wanted, and in whatever quantities she wanted. Sounds like freedom, doesn't it? But wait—according to her testimony, she wasn't free at all. She thought she would be free, but her freedom was short-lived. Instead of being free, she ended up in "bondage to food," gained sixty-five unwanted pounds, and became depressed.

When this woman discovered the Truth that "true freedom comes from obedience," and when she acted on that truth, her bondage was shattered.

6. "GOD SHOULD FIX MY PROBLEMS."

This way of thinking is deceptive on two counts. First, it reduces

God to a cosmic genie who exists to please and serve us—a hired servant who comes running to wait on us every time we ring the bell. This lie sets us up for disillusionment and disappointment with God: If we have any problems that haven't been fixed, then apparently God has not come through for us.

Second, it suggests that the goal in life is to be free from all problems—to get rid of everything that is difficult or unpleasant. Our society is conditioned to think that we should not have to live with problems—that every problem must be "fixed."

- Have a headache? Take Tylenol.
- Don't like your boss? Quit and get another job.
- Don't like your pastor's style of preaching? Find another church.
- Can't afford a newer car? Borrow.
- Men don't notice you? Flirt a bit and dress in a way that attracts their attention.
- Your husband is insensitive, addicted to sports, and doesn't romance you like he did when you were dating? Find a man at work (or at church) who cares and is willing to listen.

For many people, "Christianity" is nothing more than another way to get their problems solved. Just pray and believe in God, and you'll have plenty of money in the bank, your friend will be cured of cancer, you won't be lonely anymore, your marriage will be salvaged, your rebellious children will get right with God, you'll get instant victory over sin so you won't have to struggle with bad habits anymore, and you will be happy and healthy.

In "Holly's" case, believing this lie affected the way she dealt with the issue of overeating:

I had a problem with food and my weight. I prayed all the time for God to deliver me. But my prayers and my motives were selfish. I wanted to look good on the outside. I wanted instant results, and I did not want to sacrifice anything or work too hard for it. My prayer went like this, "Lord, I'm in a rut. I keep trying to have willpower, but I don't. Please fix this. Give me Your power to overcome this problem." But it was all in vain.

This deceptive way of thinking explains why a lot of Christian women are angry, bitter, and frustrated with life. They thought that if they accepted Jesus and went to church and tried to live a "good Christian life," they wouldn't have all these problems. Living an obedient life does spare us from many problems that are the natural consequences of a life lived apart from God and His ways. But that does not mean that those who follow Christ will be exempt from problems.

The Truth is, life is hard. We live in a fallen world. Even those who have been redeemed live in earthly bodies and have to deal with the realities of temptation, sin (both our own and others'), disease, loss, pain, and death. Becoming a Christian—even being a mature, godly Christian—does not wrap us up in some sort of celestial cocoon where we are immune to pain. Not until God makes a new heaven and new earth will we be totally free from the ravages of sin. Until then, there will be tears, sorrows, pressures, and problems.

But—and here's the good news—God is not removed or detached from our problems. He doesn't just sit up in heaven and watch to see if we will manage to survive. No, the God of the Bible is "a very present help in trouble" (Psalm 46:1 KJV). That doesn't mean He waves a magic wand and makes all our problems disappear; it does mean He uses pressures and problems to mold and shape our lives and to make us like His Son Jesus, who "learned obedience from what he suffered" (Hebrews 5:8).

We want God to fix all our problems. God says instead, "I have a purpose for your problems. I want to use your problems to change you and to reveal My grace and power to the world." That is the Truth—and the Truth will set you free.

COUNTERING LIES WITH THE TRUTH

THE LIE	THE TRUTH
1. GOD IS NOT REALLY GOOD.	• God is good, and everything He does is good. • God never makes mistakes.
2. GOD DOESN'T LOVE ME.	• God's love for me is infinite and unconditional. • I don't have to perform to earn God's love or favor. • God always has my best interests at heart.
3. GOD IS JUST LIKE MY FATHER.	• God is exactly what He has revealed Himself to be in His Word. • God is infinitely more wise and loving than any earthly father could ever be.
4. GOD IS NOT REALLY ENOUGH.	• God is enough. If I have Him, I have all I need.
5. GOD'S WAYS ARE TOO RESTRICTIVE.	• God's ways are best. • God's restrictions are always for my good. • Resisting or rebelling against God's ways brings conflict and heartache.
6. GOD SHOULD FIX MY PROBLEMS.	• Life is hard. • God is more concerned about glorifying Himself and changing me than about solving all my problems. • God has an eternal purpose He is fulfilling in the midst of my problems. • God wants to use my problems as part of His sanctifying process in my life. • No matter what problem I am facing, God's grace is sufficient for me.

According to James 1:21–25, it is not enough to hear the Truth. We must obey the Truth and allow it to become a part of the way we think and live. If we fail to do what we know, we are foolish and self-deceived. If we obey the Truth, we will be blessed.

One of the most important parts of this book is the "Making It Personal" section at the end of chapters 2–9. Before going on to the next chapter, take time to respond to the Truth you have just read. (You may wish to write your answers to these questions in a separate journal. Leave room at the end of each section to record additional insights and Scriptures you discover in the days ahead about each area of Truth addressed in this book.)

1. AGREE with God.

What lies have you believed about God?

_____

_____

2. ACCEPT responsibility.

How has believing those lies manifested itself in the way you live (e.g., attitudes, actions)?

_____

_____

3. AFFIRM the Truth.

Read aloud each of the Truths listed on page 59. Which of these truths do you particularly need to embrace at this time?

_____

Renew your mind (your thinking) by the Word of God. Read the following passages aloud. What do these verses reveal about the character of God and His heart toward His children?

Psalm 100:5

_____

Psalm 23

_____

Psalm 121

_____

Romans 8:28–39

_____

4. ACT on the Truth.

What specific step(s) of action do you need to take to align your life with the Truth you have seen about God?

_____

_____

5. ASK God to help you walk in the Truth.

Father, I acknowledge that You are good and that everything You do is good. Thank You that You don't make mistakes and that You can be trusted with every detail of this universe and of my life. By faith, I accept that You have my best interests at heart and that You are always working to fulfill Your perfect plan in my life and in the lives of those I love. Please forgive me for the times I have doubted Your wisdom, Your goodness, or Your love. I confess that I know so little of You and Your ways and that my view of You is often flawed and not according to Truth. Please teach me to know and love and trust You as You really are. In Jesus' name. Amen.

CHAPTER THREE

LIES WOMEN BELIEVE... ABOUT THEMSELVES

Dear diary,

These past few weeks have been the hardest of my life. I really wish there were someone I could to talk to. Adam and I haven't exactly been on the best of terms since we had to move. I don't know if he'll ever trust me again. In a way, I can't blame him. I've really wrecked his life. I feel so stupid. Adam just doesn't understand the effect that Serpent had on me. He was so irresistible—I felt like I couldn't help myself.

I keep reliving that moment when I first looked down and realized I was naked. Then I glanced over at Adam and realized he was thinking the same thing. For the first time since we met, I couldn't look him in the eyes. We had never before felt awkward around each other. Now we feel that way a lot of the time. Even though God gave us real clothes to replace those useless fig leaves, I still feel so . . . exposed—not just on the outside, but even more, on the inside.

I never used to think about how I looked to Adam. I always knew that he loved me and thought I was the most beautiful thing God had ever made. Now I find myself wondering if he really loves me and finds me attractive. Does he wish God hadn't given me to him?

Several months ago, one of my eyes became extremely irritated and I began to have problems wearing my contact lens. At first, I assumed I was having an allergy attack, which I tried to treat with allergy medication. However, the problem with my eye persisted. Because of the irritation, I could not see through the lens clearly; my vision was distorted. The irritation became so great that I had to remove the lens for a few days until I could get an appointment with my eye doctor.

When he examined my eye, he explained that I was not having a problem with allergies; further, the problem was not with my eye itself but with the contact lens. Somehow, the lens had been damaged—the curve had been flattened and the misshapen lens was rubbing against my eye and creating an irritation. In order to restore my vision, the damaged lens had to be replaced with a new one.

What we believe about God is crucial because it affects what we believe about everything else. A distorted or damaged view of God will distort the way we see everything and everyone around us. Frequently we fail to realize that what is causing the irritation and turmoil within our souls is not the people or the circumstances we think are annoying us; rather, the problem is that we are seeing things through a damaged lens.

One of the areas that is particularly impacted by our view of God is our view of ourselves. If we do not see Him as He really is— if we believe things about Him that are not true—invariably, we will have a distorted view of ourselves.

If we have an impoverished view of God, we will become impoverished ourselves. If we have constructed in our minds a god who is weak and impotent and not in control of every detail of the universe, we will see ourselves as being helpless and will be overwhelmed by the storms and circumstances around us. If our god is worthless, we will see ourselves as being worthless. If we have believed lies about God, we will also believe lies about ourselves. Lies such as . . .

7. "I'M NOT WORTH ANYTHING."

More than 42 percent of the women we surveyed indicated that this is a lie they have believed. It is a powerful lie, as you can see from some of their testimonies:

Feeling inferior has been a lifelong struggle. Many times it has caused me to withdraw from relationships, even though I am a people person and outgoing.

I feel the need to have constant reassurance from those around me of my value because I feel worthless! If people knew me, they would agree.

Because of the hurt in my marriage, I felt that I was useless and that nobody, not even God, could love me. I just didn't measure up, and since I have always felt that I had to be perfect to be loved, then obviously God would not love me either.

In many cases, these feelings of worthlessness are the result of believing things we have heard from others, especially in childhood:

I was told as a child that I was worthless as tits on a bear. I soon believed that I was. I still have trouble with this at times.

*I believed that I would never be anybody in this world because
that is what I heard when I was growing up. People saw me as a
retarded person who didn't know anything. At that time I believed
it. I used to lock myself up and wouldn't want to do anything with
anybody. I have believed all of my life that I would never have any
good friends or family and that I would rot away with the suffering and pain that I went through most of my life.*

The problem is that our view of ourselves and our sense of worth
are often determined by the input and opinions of others. Sometimes
the input of others is accurate and helpful. But not always. If, for some
reason, the person we are listening to is looking through a defective
"lens," his or her vision will be distorted. Some of us have lived all
our lives in an emotional prison because we have accepted what a
false, "broken" mirror said to us about ourselves.

Even when the input is, in and of itself, true, the Deceiver can use
that data to put us in bondage. For example, a playmate may accu-
rately observe to a six-year-old girl, "You're fat!" That little girl will
one day find herself in bondage if she grows up drawing false con-
clusions based on that comment: "I'm fat. Therefore, . . .

- I'll always be fat";
- nobody could ever like me or want me to be her friend";
- I'm worthless";
- I have to be the life of the party in order to be liked or accepted by others."

Sometimes, a single sentence heard as a child can haunt and plague
a person for years. That is what happened to "Mindy":

*I have a memory of being about six and being told I had no right
to live and I should have never been born. I don't remember who*

66

said it, but I do remember my mother just standing there and not doing anything about it. I became very withdrawn, and it was extremely difficult to talk to people.

By the time I was to start seventh grade, it was decided I belonged in special education. I was accepted into the classes, but there wasn't room, so I went to the normal junior high school. I never believed I belonged there.

Until this weekend, I have believed I was stupid, not normal, and I should be locked away somewhere. In junior high, I had no friends, and people went out of their way to hurt me. As a result, I withdrew even more, became very depressed, and wanted to go to sleep and never wake up.

This story poignantly illustrates the progression we have seen that leads to bondage. First, as a child, this woman was told a terrible, destructive lie. She listened to the lie; then, rather than countering the lie with the Truth, she dwelt on the lie until she believed it was actually true. Ultimately, she acted on the lie ("I withdrew . . ."), until she found herself in bondage to the lie: "[I] became very depressed, and wanted to go to sleep and never wake up."

What we believe about ourselves determines how we live. If we believe and act on lies, we will end up in bondage, as illustrated by these two testimonies:

For the longest time I thought I was not worth anything. Even after I was saved, I thought I was equal to pond scum. This threw me into depression. I began to isolate myself, and as a result, was not living the life of joy that God had intended for me.

"I am not worth anything" is a lie I believed. I have always struggled with this lie and with a constant "need" for the approval of others. It got to the point of being maddening—trying to please

everyone, trying to have the appearance of what I thought I should look like.

❦❦

These testimonies are not unique. I find that many women to-day are desperately seeking for affirmation; they are driven to gain the approval of others. It's as if they were trying to balance the scales of the negative input they have received from others. But, in most cases, no number of positive "strokes" can outweigh those negative, hurt-ful expressions that have led them to believe they are worthless. No amount of affirmation is enough. They can get one hundred com-pliments about how they look or what they have done, but let one family member offer a criticism, and they are devastated. Why? Be-cause they are letting others determine their worth.

There is a wonderful verse in 1 Peter that shows us how Jesus' sense of worth was determined, not by what others thought of Him—good or bad—but by the Truth as expressed by His heavenly Father: He was "rejected by men but chosen by God and precious to him" (2:4). Jesus was *rejected by men*—those He had created for Himself, those He loved and for whom He laid down His life. But that is not what determined His value. He was *chosen by God;* that is what made Him precious; that is what determined His worth.

It is conceivable that someone who did not recognize or appre-ciate fine art would toss a masterpiece into the trash. Would that make the painting any less valuable? Not at all. The true worth of the art would be seen when an art collector spotted the painting and said, "That is a priceless piece, and I am willing to pay any amount to ac-quire it."

When God sent His only Son, Jesus, to this earth to bear your sin and mine on the cross, He put a price tag on us—He declared the value of our soul to be greater than the value of the whole world. Whose opinion are you going to accept? Believing a lie will put you in bondage. Believing the Truth will set you free.

8. "I NEED TO LEARN TO LOVE MYSELF."

"Low self-esteem" is one of the most common diagnoses of our day. Mental health professionals diagnose it in their clients; teachers diagnose it in their students; pastors diagnose it in their counselees; parents diagnose it in their children; and countless people diagnose it in themselves.

"You need to learn to love yourself" is the world's prescription for those who are plagued with a sense of worthlessness. It has become a popular mantra of pop psychology and of a culture filled with people obsessed with finding ways to feel better about themselves.

One religious catalog offers an attractive afghan with a "Love Yourself" acrostic:

Let go of the shoulds in your life.
Open up to the miracle of you.
Value your uniqueness.
Explore your dreams and passions.

Yield to life—go with the flow.
Obey the voice of your spirit.
Unwind—get cozy and comfy.
Renew yourself—body and soul.
Surround yourself with caring people.
Express yourself—be true to you.
Linger longer at what you enjoy.
Feel God's special love for you.

Another catalog offers a "Magical Nightshirt," with the following message printed backwards, so the wearer can read it to herself by looking in the mirror: "I am a precious, wondrous, special, unique, giving, rare, valuable, whole, sacred, total, complete, entitled, worthy, and deserving person." The nightshirt is "meant to remind you just how precious and unique you are."

As with much deception, the lies represented in these advertisements are not the polar opposite of the Truth; rather, they are distortions of the Truth. According to God's Word, the Truth is that we were created in the image of God, that He loves us, and that we are precious to Him. However, we do not bestow that worth on ourselves. Nor do we experience the fullness of God's love by telling ourselves how lovable we are. To the contrary, Jesus taught that it is in losing our lives that we find our lives. The message of self-love puts people on a lonely, one-way path to misery.

How often have we heard someone say, "I've never liked myself," or "She just can't love herself"? According to the Scripture, the Truth is that we do love ourselves—immensely. When Jesus tells us to love our neighbors as ourselves, the point is not that we need to learn to love ourselves so that we can love others. Jesus is saying we need to give others the same attention and care we naturally give ourselves.

If I get a toothache, I immediately look for a way to identify the problem and get rid of it. If I didn't "love myself," I would ignore the pain. But when someone else has a toothache, it is easy to be indifferent to his need—that's his problem. We naturally love ourselves; we do not naturally love others.

The same point is made in Ephesians 5, where Paul says that husbands are to "love their wives as [they instinctively love] their own bodies.... After all, *no one ever hated his own body,* but he feeds and cares for it" (vv. 28–29, italics added).

We are constantly looking out for ourselves, deeply sensitive to our own feelings and needs, always conscious of how things and people affect us. The reason some of us get hurt so easily is not because we hate ourselves but because we love ourselves! We want to be accepted, cherished, and treated well. If we did not care so much about ourselves, we would not be so concerned about being rejected, neglected, or mistreated.

The fact is, we do not hate ourselves, nor do we need to learn to love ourselves. We need to learn how to deny ourselves, so we can do that which does not come naturally—to truly love God and others. Our malady is not "low self-esteem," nor is it how we view ourselves; rather, it is our low view of God. Our problem isn't so much a "poor self-image" as it is a "poor God-image." Our need is not to love ourselves more but to receive His incredible love for us and to accept His design and purpose for our lives.

Once we have received His love, we will not have to compare ourselves to others; we will not focus on "self" at all. Instead, we will become channels of His love to others.

9. "I CAN'T HELP THE WAY I AM."

This is another lie that puts many people in lifelong bondage. It is a lie we have all believed at one time or another. Perhaps you can relate to one of these women:

The lie I believed was: "You'll be just like your parents—it's hereditary—you can't help it." My dad was a minister while I was growing up. He and my mom turned away from God and the church. I believed a person could not remain faithful to God forever —that because my parents didn't, I wouldn't either.

I have excused my laziness and lack of discipline, believing that I cannot help the way that I am.

I believed I had a weight problem because all my dad's family is fat. I have their body type, so I am always going to struggle. No use trying—it just comes back anyway. Therefore, I was placing blame on them for my bondage to food.

We see things about ourselves we wish were different or that we know are not pleasing to the Lord. But rather than accept personal responsibility for our own choices, attitudes, and behavior, we have 101 reasons for why we are the way we are:

- "Our house is so tiny, everything gets on my nerves."
- "My job is so stressful, I can't help being irritable with my kids when I get home."
- "It's that time of the month."
- "My hormones are going crazy."
- "I'm so exhausted; I just can't function."
- "My family never dealt with problems; we just stuffed everything inside and pretended like nothing was wrong. To this day, I can't really confront issues."
- "My parents never affirmed me, and I've never been able to feel loved."
- "My mother and her mother were both manic-depressive—I guess it just runs in our family."
- "My mother was never a real mother to me—I've never had a model to show me how to raise my kids."
- "I had an abusive childhood; I've never been able to trust people."
- "My ex-husband constantly put me down; he destroyed my self-esteem."

The implication of all these statements is that others have made us the way we are—that we are merely victims, reacting to wounds inflicted on us by others.

However, as we reflect on Eve's story, we discover that it was not parents or a mate or a child who accounted for the first woman's misery. It was not a man who ruined her life—contrary to the insistence of modern-day feminism that men are largely responsible for our problems as women. Nor could Eve blame her environment. In fact, talk about an environment where it should have been easy to succeed and be happy! Eve and her husband had no financial problems, no problems at work, no pollution, no unpleasant neighbors, and no weeds to pull; they didn't even have in-law problems!

Eve had no one and nothing outside herself to blame for the troubles she encountered in her marriage, her family, and her environment. Her problems began within herself. Eve made a simple, personal choice—there was no one but herself to blame. That choice placed her in bondage and brought untold misery to her life, her family, and every generation that was to follow.

This lie—"I can't help the way I am"—makes us into helpless victims of other people and outside circumstances. The suggestion is that someone or something else is responsible for who we are—that we have no more control over who we are and what we do than a marionette does. We somehow believe that we are destined to be controlled by whoever or whatever is pulling our strings.

This lie leaves us without hope that we can ever be any different. Satan knows that if we believe we can't help the way we are, we will never change. We will go on living in bondage. If we believe we are doomed to fail, to keep on sinning, or to be miserable, we *will* fail, we *will* keep on sinning, and we *will* always be unhappy, frustrated women.

The Truth is that we *do* have a choice. We are responsible for our own choices. We can be changed by the power of God's Spirit. Once we know and embrace the Truth, we can break free from the chains of our past, our circumstances, and even deeply ingrained habit patterns.

🍎 10. "I HAVE MY RIGHTS."

"Certain inalienable rights" . . . "Have it your way!" . . . "You've got a right—to chicken done right!" From the Declaration of Independence to fast- food chicken, "I've got a right" has become the watch cry of Western civilization. In our generation, this has been particularly true of women.

The modern-day feminist movement was birthed and has been sustained by persuading women to march and clamor for "rights": the right to vote; the right to be free from the shackles of housework; the right to equal employment opportunities; the right to equal wages; the right to control our own bodies; the right to say what we want to say, to do what we want to do, to be what we want to be; the right to be free from a husband's name and from every other form of "male domination."

Women have been told that demanding their rights was the ticket to happiness and freedom. After all, "If you don't stand up for your rights, no one else will!" However, I am convinced that the claiming of rights has produced much, if not most, of the unhappiness women experience today. Day after day, I hear from women who admit that "standing up for their rights" has not always brought the promised benefits:

"I have my rights" has caused many unnecessary arguments, which led to unhappiness.

When I stand up for my rights and demand my way, I am temporarily happy, but the pit of despair soon follows.

The fact is, successful relationships and healthy cultures are not built on the *claiming* of rights but on the *yielding* of rights. Even our traffic laws reflect this principle. You'll never see a sign that says, "You have the right of way." Instead, the signs instruct us to "Yield" the right of way. That is how traffic flows best; it is also how life works best.

Nonetheless, the idea of claiming rights is in the air we breathe. The turmoil and rebellion of the 1960s was birthed out of a philosophy that promoted rights. This philosophy has permeated our Christian culture. It creeps into our conversations. It has shaped the way we view all of life. Today it is assumed that . . .

- you have a right to be happy;
- you have a right to be understood;
- you have a right to be loved;
- you have a right to a certain standard of living, to an equitable wage, and to decent benefits;
- you have a right to a good marriage;
- you have a right to companionship and romance;
- you have a right to be treated with respect in the workplace;
- you have a right to be valued by your husband and appreciated by your children;
- you have a right to time off and a certain number of vacation days;
- you have a right to a good night's sleep;
- you have a right to have your husband pitch in with the household chores.

And most important, if any of your rights are violated, you have a right to protest. You have a right to be angry. You have a right to be depressed. You have a right to take action. You have a right to insist on your rights!

The Old Testament prophet Jonah illustrates the natural human tendency to claim rights and become angry when those "rights" are violated. Jonah felt he had a right to dislike the pagan Ninevites. He had a right to minister where he wanted to minister. He had a right to see the Ninevites judged by God.

When God acted differently from the way Jonah thought He should, "Jonah was greatly displeased and became angry" (Jonah 4:1). He became so angry that he begged God to take his life. His suicidal thoughts were the result of an emotional temper tantrum.

When the Lord responded to Jonah, He didn't sympathize with Jonah's wounded feelings; He didn't try to stroke Jonah's ego. Instead, He confronted the pouting prophet with the issue of rights: "The LORD replied, 'Have you any right to be angry?'" (v. 4).

Jonah refused to answer the question.

Instead, he went to the outskirts of Nineveh, built a temporary shelter, and sat down to wait and see if God would change His mind and destroy the city. Out of His loving-kindness and mercy, "God provided a vine and made it grow up over Jonah to give shade for his head to ease his discomfort, *and Jonah was very happy about the vine*" (v. 6, italics added).

Can you see how Jonah's emotions were controlled by whether or not he thought his rights were being fulfilled? When God was merciful to the pagans Jonah detested, Jonah was displeased and angry. And when God provided the convenience of a shelter from the hot, eastern sun, Jonah was happy.

His happiness was short-lived, however, for the next morning, God sent a worm that chewed the vine until it withered; then He sent a scorching wind and a hot sun to burn on Jonah, until he became faint. Once again, the depressed prophet begged to die. And once again, God challenged Jonah's rights: "Do you have a right to be angry about the vine?" (v. 9). Jonah responded, "I do. . . . I am angry enough to die" (v. 9).

Jonah felt he had the right to control his own life and environment, to have things go the way he wanted them to go, and to be angry when they didn't. His insistence on his rights caused him to be emotionally unstable, isolated, and estranged from God.

The sad thing is that Jonah's story sounds a lot like my own at times. All too often, I find myself annoyed and perturbed when things don't go *my way*. A decision someone makes at the office, a rude driver on the freeway, a long line at the checkout counter, a thoughtless word spoken by a family member, a minor offense (real or perceived) by a friend, someone who fails to come through on a commitment, a phone call that wakes me when I have just fallen off to sleep—if I am staking out my rights, even the smallest violation of those rights can leave me feeling and acting moody, uptight, and angry.

The only way to get off that kind of spiritual and emotional roller coaster is to *yield* all my rights to the One who ultimately holds all rights. That is the Truth—and the Truth will set us free.

11. "PHYSICAL BEAUTY MATTERS MORE THAN INNER BEAUTY."

This message is one our culture preaches in earnest to girls and women, beginning in earliest childhood. It comes at us from virtually every angle: television, movies, music, magazines, books, and advertisements. In nearly perfect unison, they paint for us a picture of what really matters. And what matters most for women, they insist, is beauty—physical beauty. Even parents, siblings, teachers, and friends sometimes add unwittingly to the chorus: "darling" children get oohs, aahs, and doting attention, while less attractive, overweight, or gangly children may be the objects of unkind comments, indifference, or even overt rejection.

I believe that our preoccupation with external appearance goes back to the first woman. Do you remember what it was that appealed to Eve about the forbidden fruit?

> When the woman saw that the fruit of the tree was good for food and *pleasing to the eye,* and also desirable for gaining wisdom, she took some and ate it.
>
> *Genesis 3:6, italics added*

The fruit had a functional appeal (it was "good for food"); it also appealed to her desire for wisdom. But equally important was the fact that it was "pleasing to the eye"—it was physically attractive. The Enemy succeeded in getting the woman to value physical appearance more highly than less visible qualities, such as trust and obedience. The problem wasn't that the fruit was "beautiful"—God had made it that way. Nor was it wrong for Eve to enjoy and appreciate the beauty of God's creation. The problem was that Eve placed undue emphasis on external appearance. In doing so, she believed and acted on a lie.

The priority Eve placed on physical attractiveness became the accepted pattern for all human beings. From that moment on, she and her husband saw themselves and their physical bodies through different eyes. They became self-conscious and ashamed of their bodies—bodies that had been masterfully formed by a loving Creator. They immediately sought to cover up their bodies, afraid to risk exposure before one another.

The deception that physical beauty is to be esteemed above beauty of heart, spirit, and life leaves both men and women feeling unattractive, ashamed, embarrassed, and hopelessly flawed. Ironically, the pursuit of physical beauty is invariably an unattainable, elusive goal—always just out of reach.

Even the most glamorous, admired women admit to feeling less than beautiful. One of Hollywood's darlings, Meg Ryan, says of herself: "I think I'm kind of weird-looking. If I could change the way I look, I'd like to have longer legs, smaller feet, a smaller nose."[1]

One might ask, how much damage can it do to place inordinate value on physical, external beauty? Let's go back to our premise: What we believe ultimately determines how we live. If we believe something that is not true, sooner or later we will act on that lie; believing and acting on lies leads us into bondage.

Each of the following women *believed* something about beauty that is not true. What they *believed* impacted the way they *felt* about themselves and caused them to make *choices* that placed them in *bondage*.

By believing *that beauty is external and physical, I have never felt that I was beautiful. I was* ashamed *of the scars on my back and legs. I just have one line down both my legs and back from scoliosis. I have a straight back, but I have always felt it cost me some of my beauty.* Because I believed I was not pretty, I have been shy.

I believed that outward beauty (my body) was all that was valuable about me to anyone, especially men. I chose to take advantage of that to get the attention I so desperately craved. I became a sexual addict.

I have a beautiful sister, whom I adore, but I am plain. I have always believed *myself to be inferior and that I must perform to be accepted by others. I see the beautiful people get the breaks in life. I just accept that I won't, and* I am in bondage to my perception of my appearance.

All my life I have believed *that my self-worth was based on my appearance, and of course I never looked like the world said I should, so I have always had a low self-worth.* I developed eating disorders, am a food addict, and struggle in my marriage *with the perception that I am not attractive, and that my husband is always looking at other women who are attractive to him.*

Comparison, envy, competitiveness, promiscuity, sexual addictions, eating disorders, immodest dress, flirtatious behavior—the list of attitudes and behaviors rooted in a false view of beauty is long. What can set women free from this bondage? Only the Truth can overcome the lies we have believed. God's Word tells us the Truth about the transitory nature of physical beauty and the importance of pursuing lasting, inner beauty:

> Charm is deceptive, and beauty is fleeting; but a woman
> who fears the LORD is to be praised.
>
> *Proverbs 31:30*

> Your beauty should not come from outward adornment, such
> as braided hair and the wearing of gold jewelry and fine
> clothes. Instead, it should be that of your inner self, the un-
> fading beauty of a gentle and quiet spirit, which is of great
> worth in God's sight. For this is the way the holy women of

the past who put their hope in God
used to make themselves beautiful.

1 Peter 3:3–5

These verses do not teach, as some might think, that physical
beauty is somehow sinful, or that it is wrong to pay any attention to
our outward appearance. That is just as much a deception as the lie
that places an overemphasis on external beauty.

Nowhere does the Scripture condemn physical beauty or suggest
that the outward appearance does not matter. What is condemned is
taking pride in God-given beauty, giving excessive attention to physical beauty, or tending to physical matters while neglecting matters
of the heart.

One of Satan's strategies is to get us to move from one extreme to
another. There is a growing aversion in our culture to neatness, order-
liness, and attractiveness in dress and physical appearance. I sometimes
find myself wanting to say to Christian women: "Do you know who
you are? God made you a woman. Accept His gift. Don't be afraid to
be feminine and to add physical and spiritual loveliness to the setting
where He has placed you. You are a child of God. You are a part of the
bride of Christ. You belong to the King—you are royalty. Dress and
conduct yourself in a way that reflects your high and holy calling. God
has called you out of this world's system—don't let the world press
you into its mold. Don't think, dress, or act like the world; inwardly and
outwardly, let others see the difference He makes in your life."

We as Christian women should seek to reflect the beauty, order,
excellence, and grace of God through both our outward and inner
person.

The Christian wife has even more reason to find the right balance in this matter. The "virtuous wife" of Proverbs 31 is physically
fit and well dressed (vv. 17, 22). She is a compliment to her husband.

If a wife dresses in a way that is slovenly and unkempt, if she
does not take any care for her physical appearance, she reflects

negatively on her husband (and on her heavenly Bridegroom). Further, if she makes no effort to be physically attractive for her husband, you may be sure another woman out there will be standing in line to get his attention.

When the apostle Paul wrote to Timothy about how things ought to be in the church, he took time to address the way women dress. His instructions show the balance between the inner heart attitude of the woman and her outer attire and behavior. Paul exhorts women to

> adorn themselves in modest apparel, with propriety and moderation, not with braided hair or gold or pearls or costly clothing, but, which is proper for women professing godliness, with good works.

1 Timothy 2:9–10 (NKJV)

The words translated "adorn" and "modest" in this text mean "orderly, well-arranged, decent"; they speak of "harmonious arrangement."[2] The outward appearance of the Christian woman is to reflect a heart that is simple, pure, and well-ordered; her clothing and hairstyles should not be distracting or draw attention to herself by being extravagant, extreme, or indecent. In this way, she reflects the true condition of her heart and her relationship with the Lord, and she makes the Gospel attractive to the world.

FORTY AND COUNTING

No sooner had I turned forty, than I started receiving catalogs promoting products guaranteed to combat the effects of aging—they promise me younger, clearer skin; fewer wrinkles; no more dark shadows; more energy; prettier nails and hair; and improved eyesight and hearing. The implication is that, as I get older, what matters most is looking and feeling younger.

However, the fact is, I *am* getting older, and in this fallen world, that means my body is slowly deteriorating. I look in the mirror and see lines that weren't there ten years ago; I am definitely gray-headed; I have had to start using a "large print Bible"; and in spite of regular exercise and watching what I eat, I just don't have the physical stamina I had at twenty.

But I refuse to buy into the lie that those things are ultimate tragedies or that my biological clock can somehow be reversed. I am not trying to hasten my physical decline, but neither am I going to get consumed with fighting off the inevitable. As I get older, I want to focus on those things that God says matter most—things like letting His Spirit cultivate in me a gracious, wise, kind, loving heart.

Regardless of what potions, pills, or procedures I purchase, I know there is a process taking place in my physical body that will not be reversed this side of eternity. To believe otherwise is to be deceived. But I also know that "the path of the righteous is like the first gleam of dawn, shining ever brighter till the full light of day" (Proverbs 4:18). That means there is a dimension of life that can grow richer and fuller, even as our outer bodies are decaying.

The fact is, if we devote our time and energy to staying fit, trim, glamorous, and youthful looking, we may achieve those objectives—for a while. But the day will come when we will regret having neglected to cultivate that inner beauty, character, and radiance that are pleasing to God and last forever.

12. "I SHOULD NOT HAVE TO LIVE WITH UNFULFILLED LONGINGS."

This is another lie that has worked its way into the warp and woof of the way we think and live. Our society has bought into the philosophy that there is (or ought to be) a remedy (preferably quick and easy) for every unfulfilled longing.

We are encouraged to identify our longings and do whatever is necessary to get those "needs" met. Therefore . . . if you're hungry, eat. If you want something you can't afford, charge it. If you crave romance, dress or act in a way that will get men to notice you. If you're lonely, share your heart with that married man at work.

The next time you're in the grocery store, take a quick look at the women's magazines at the checkout counter. The covers are filled with offers that promise to satisfy all your longings:

- 99 Ways to Look Better, Feel Better, Enjoy Life More!
- Snack Off Weight
- Look Gorgeous When It's 100°
- 25 Secrets to Looking Young
- Indulge Yourself: Instant Long Hair; Goof-proof Self-tanning
- The Little Health Habit That Keeps You Thin, Improves Your Skin, and Ups Your Energy!
- The Easy Life: Fun Jobs, Cool Dresses, Wild Fantasies, and Smart Solutions

Somewhere, somehow, there is a way to fulfill your longings—it may be

- a how-to book;
- a romance novel;
- a trip to the mall;
- a cruise;
- a new hairstyle, wardrobe, house, perfume, job, or husband;
- a deep-dish pizza dripping with melted cheese.

At best, this way of thinking has left many women still unfulfilled, still groping, still searching for something to fill the inner emptiness.

At its worst, this deception has caused enormous heartache and bondage. It is at the heart of much anxiety, resentment, and depression. This lie has led countless women to trade in their virginity for a warm body and the promise of companionship. It has led married women to seek fulfillment in the arms of a man at work who claimed to care about her feelings. It has led many young people down the aisle of a church to exchange wedding vows for all the wrong reasons. And it has led a high percentage of those same couples down the aisle of a divorce court—all in an effort to satisfy their deep, unfulfilled inner longings.

"Carmen" shares where this lie led her:

❧ ❧

Believing that I should not have to live with unfulfilled longings, I got what I wanted when I wanted it. Clothes, trips to Europe, or weekends away—put on credit cards or financed some way, until I had approximately $7,000–10,000 debt by the time I was twenty-two. The other thing I desired and felt like I needed now was a man—consequently, I would date men I was not even interested in or men that I knew only wanted to sleep with me. To have dates, I would occasionally go ahead and have sex just to feel accepted.

❧ ❧

"Eileen's" story demonstrates the depths of emotional and personal destruction that can result from believing this lie:

❧ ❧

I was not sexually fulfilled in my marriage, and I believed it was my husband's fault. I blamed him and sought another man to satisfy me sexually. I called it love, knowing it was lust, but believed it was my right, that my husband owed it to me to have sexual fulfillment. It was great for a while, but when it unraveled, the guilt, the shame, and the destruction left a patch of hurt and pain too great and not worth whatever pleasure I may have felt for such a brief moment.

❧ ❧

What is the Truth that sets us free from the bondage of this deception?

First, we have to recognize that *we will always have unfulfilled longings this side of heaven* (Romans 8:23). In fact, if we could have all our longings fulfilled down here, we would easily be satisfied with staying here, and our hearts would never long for a better place.

It is important to understand that our inner longings are not necessarily sinful in and of themselves. What *is* wrong is demanding that those longings be fulfilled here and now, or insisting on meeting those longings in illegitimate ways.

God created the sexual drive. It is not wrong to fulfill that drive, as long as it is fulfilled in God's timing and in God's way—within the marriage covenant. However, the world tells us that if we have a drive for sexual intimacy, we have every right to fulfill it—regardless of how, when, where, or with whom.

Likewise, it is not wrong to have physical hunger; nor is it wrong to eat. What is wrong is when we stuff ourselves in an effort to satisfy emotional and spiritual longings.

Until God provides the legitimate context to fulfill our longings, we must learn to be content with unfulfilled longings.

The second Truth is that *the deepest longings of our hearts cannot be filled by any created person or thing*. This is one of the most liberating Truths I have discovered in my own pilgrimage. For years, I looked to people and circumstances to make me happy. Time after time, when they failed to come through, I would find myself disgruntled and disappointed.

The Truth is, every created thing is guaranteed to disappoint us. Things can burn or break or be stolen or get lost. People can move or change or fail or die. It took the loss of some of my dearest loved ones some years ago to awaken me to the Truth that I would always live in a state of disappointment if I was looking to people to satisfy me at the core of my being.

I have talked with many single young women—some of them godly, committed believers—who have shared with me their struggle with loneliness. I remind them that marriage is not necessarily a cure for loneliness—I have met plenty of married women who struggle with a deep sense of loneliness and isolation. The fact is, there is

no man on the face of the earth who can satisfy the deepest longings of a woman's heart—God has made us in such a way that we
can never be truly satisfied with anything or anyone less than Himself (Psalms 16:11; 34:8–10).

Whether married or single, we must recognize that it is not wrong
to have unfulfilled longings—they do not make us any less spiritual.
We must learn to accept those longings, surrender them to God, and
look to Him to meet the deepest needs of our hearts.

We have seen that a flawed view of God results in a flawed view
of ourselves, and that deception in either of these crucial areas affects the way we live. Inevitably, believing lies about God or about
ourselves will also lead to being deceived about sin.

COUNTERING LIES WITH THE TRUTH

THE LIE	THE TRUTH
7. I'M NOT WORTH ANYTHING.	• My value is not determined by what others think of me or what I think of myself. My value is determined by how God views me. • To God, my soul is worth more than the price of the whole world. • If I am a child of God, I am God's cherished possession and treasure.
8. I NEED TO LEARN TO LOVE MYSELF.	• By faith, I need to receive God's love for me. • I already love myself. I need to deny myself and let God love others through me.
9. I CAN'T HELP THE WAY I AM.	• If I am a child of God, I can choose to obey God. • I am responsible for my own choices. • I can be changed through the power of God's Spirit.
10. I HAVE MY RIGHTS.	• Claiming rights will put me in bondage. • Yielding rights will set me free.
11. PHYSICAL BEAUTY MATTERS MORE THAN INNER BEAUTY.	• At best, physical beauty is temporal and fleeting. • The beauty that matters most to God is that of my inner spirit and character.
12. I SHOULD NOT HAVE TO LIVE WITH UNFULFILLED LONGINGS.	• I will always have unfulfilled longings this side of heaven. • The deepest longings of my heart cannot be filled by any created person or thing. • If I will accept them, unfulfilled longings will increase my longing for God and for heaven.

1. AGREE with God.

What lies have you believed about yourself?

_____

_____

2. ACCEPT responsibility.

How has believing those lies manifested itself in the way you live (e.g., attitudes, actions)?

_____

_____

3. AFFIRM the Truth.

Read aloud each of the Truths listed on page 87. Which of these Truths do you particularly need to embrace at this time?

_____

Renew your mind (your thinking) by the Word of God. Read the following passages aloud. What do these verses reveal about how God views you?

Psalm 139:13–18

_____

Ephesians 1:3–8

_____

Romans 5:6–8

_____

Romans 8:1–2, 13, 15–17

_____

4. ACT on the Truth.

What specific step(s) of action do you need to take to align your life with the Truth you have seen about yourself?

_____

_____

5. ASK God to help you walk in the Truth.

Father, Thank You for pursuing a relationship with me when I was estranged from You and had rejected Your love. I know that apart from You, there is nothing good in me. Thank You for not giving up on me. Thank You for loving me with an infinite, unconditional love. Thank You for giving Your Son to take the penalty for my sin and to die in my place. Thank You for choosing me to be Your child and for making me Your cherished possession. Thank You for sending Your Holy Spirit to live in me and for making my body Your dwelling place. Thank You for Your commitment to change me and to make me like Jesus. Help me to cooperate with You in that process. Please produce in me the beauty—the heart, character, and responses—of the Lord Jesus. In His name I pray. Amen.

CHAPTER FOUR

LIES WOMEN BELIEVE... ABOUT SIN

Dear diary,

It's been six months since we left Eden; I wish we could put this all behind us. Adam still blames me for the whole mess. I know I shouldn't have listened to the Serpent. But Adam was right there with me. Why didn't he do something? And it's not like he didn't eat the fruit, too.

At the time, I honestly didn't think it was such a big deal. Now, I have this overwhelming sense of guilt—how could I have done this to God after all He had done for us? Will we ever be able to have the same kind of relationship we used to have? Whenever I try to talk to Him, I feel like there is this great big wall between us.

One thing I hadn't counted on was how totally unnatural it would be to obey God once I ate that fruit. For example . . . until that day, whenever I got hungry, I would eat; when I was full, I stopped. Now I have this constant craving for food—once I start eating, I can't stop, even when I know I should.

That's not the only area where I get out of control; my tongue gets me in so much trouble, especially on days like yesterday—it was that time of the month, and I wasn't feeling well. I found my-self snapping at Adam about every little thing. I hate it when I act this way. I don't like being moody and uptight. But sometimes I feel like I just can't help myself.

When the Romeros first got Sally as a family pet, she was only one foot long. Eight years later, she had grown to eleven-and-a-half feet and weighed eighty pounds. Then on July 20, 1993, Sally, a Burmese python, attacked fifteen-year-old Derek, strangling the teenager until he suffocated to death.

In one fatal moment, the creature that had seemed so docile and harmless was exposed as a deadly beast. The "pet" the unsuspecting family had brought into their home, cared for, and nurtured turned on them and proved to be a destroyer. In a sense, no one should have been surprised at the turn of events, for in the end, the python merely did what was its nature to do.

So it is with sin. Though it may entertain us, play with us, sleep with us, and amuse us, its nature never changes. Inevitably, it will al-ways rise up to bite and devour those who befriend it.

All deception is deadly. But no lies are more deadly than those Sa-tan tells us about God and about sin. He tries to convince us that God is not who He says He is and that sin is not what He says it is. Satan paints a picture that diminishes both the God-likeness of God and the sinfulness of sin. He makes God out to be not so good and sin out to be not so evil.

Modern technology has made it possible to enhance photographs in such dramatic ways that the ugliest image can be made to look beautiful. That is exactly what Satan does with sin. He cleverly en-hances the image to make something that is hideous and deformed appear to be a work of beauty and art.

But dressing sin up cannot change its essential nature. Like the python that seemed so innocent and tranquil, there comes a point when its true, deadly nature is exposed.

Satan used deception in the Garden to pull off a revolt that turned out to be more costly than anyone could have imagined. The lies he tells us today are essentially the same as the lies he told the first woman.

13. "I CAN SIN AND GET AWAY WITH IT."

This may be the most fundamental lie Satan tells us about sin. God had said to Adam, "If you eat the fruit of this tree, you will die." The command was clear: "Don't eat." The consequence for disobedience was equally clear: "You will die."

After Satan raised a question in Eve's mind about the goodness of God in giving such a mandate and whether God in fact had the right to control her life, he proceeded to challenge the consequence. He did so with a direct, frontal attack on the word of God: " *'You will not surely die,'* the serpent said to the woman" (Genesis 3:4, italics added).

Three times in Psalm 10 the writer indicates that the reason people disobey God is that they believe they can get away with it:

> He says to himself, "Nothing will shake me;
> I'll always be happy and never have trouble." . . .
> He says to himself, "God has forgotten;
> he covers his face and never sees." . . .
> Why does the wicked man revile God?
> Why does he say to himself,
> "He won't call me to account"?
>
> *Psalm 10:6, 11, 13*

93

The Enemy causes us to believe that

• "there will be no judgment on my sin";
• "I won't reap what I sow";
• "the choices I make today will not have consequences";
• "I can play with fire and not get burned."

As with many other lies, we don't consciously believe these things—we may even intellectually reject this kind of thinking. But when we choose to sin, it is invariably because we think we can get away with it. And so we choose to eat that second dessert, even though we're already stuffed—not stopping to consider that . . .

• in a few hours, we will feel bloated and sick to our stomach;
• tomorrow when we step on the scales, we will be kicking ourselves for yielding;
• a series of such choices will likely lead to excessive weight gain, resulting in guilt, frustration, and depression;
• overeating may well lead to heartburn, diabetes, a stroke, or heart failure;
• lack of restraint in one area of our lives makes us more vulnerable to lack of discipline in other, more major areas;
• the indulgence we excuse in moderation may well produce in our children a harvest of extreme indulgence.

We entertain ourselves with reading material, movies, TV programs, and music that reflect worldly philosophies and legitimize profanity, immodesty, and immoral behavior, never stopping to contemplate that in so doing . . .

• we are desensitizing our conscience and developing a tolerance for sin;
• we are increasing our appetite for sin and diminishing our hunger for holiness;

- we are erecting a barrier in our fellowship with God;
- we are programming our minds to think the world's way (and how we think will ultimately determine how we live);
- we are increasing the likelihood that we will actually act out the things we are seeing and hearing;
- we are developing an unbiblical view of sexuality that may ultimately rob us of our virginity or destroy our marriage;
- we are increasing the likelihood that our children and grand-children will become profane and immoral.

We choose to hold a grudge against someone who has wronged us, ignoring the fact that sooner or later, our bitterness will ...

- destroy our capacity to think rationally;
- make us miserable and emotionally unstable;
- affect our bodies in such ways as chronic tiredness, loss of energy, headaches, muscle tension, and intestinal disorders;
- keep us from being able to experience God's forgiveness for our sins;
- make us hard to live with and cause people not to want to be around us.

We let ourselves get too close to a kind, thoughtful man at work or someone we meet in a chat room, refusing to let ourselves be-lieve that ...

- we are planting seeds of infidelity in our minds and emotions;
- we are making it impossible for our own husband to please us because reality cannot compete with fantasy;
- we may well end up destroying his marriage and ours;
- we may well wreck the lives of our children;

- even if we don't commit adultery with him, we are setting ourselves up for future moral failure;
- we may end up hopelessly estranged from our mate, our children, our in-laws, and our God.

We must keep reminding ourselves that Satan is a liar. The things God calls "sin," Satan tells us are

fun	*no big deal*
safe	*meeting our needs*
innocent	*unavoidable*
desirable	

- The Truth is that sin is dangerous, deadly, and destructive.
- The Truth is that we *will* reap what we sow.
- The Truth is that every choice we make today *will* have consequences.
- The Truth is that if we play with fire, we *will* get burned.
- The Truth is that "sin, when it is full-grown, gives birth to death" (James 1:15).

Unfortunately, most people simply don't make the connection between their natural, fleshly choices and the consequences in their lives, their marriages, their children, their health, and their relationship with God and others.

THE DELIGHTS OF SIN

Satan's deception goes a step further than telling us we can get away with sin. In the Garden, he suggested to Eve, "Not only can you disobey God and avoid negative consequences; there are also some definite benefits you will experience if you eat this fruit."

For God knows that when
you eat of it your eyes will be opened,
and you will be like God, knowing good and evil.

Genesis 3:5

He was saying, in effect, that whatever consequences you may reap are worth the pleasure and benefits you will receive from "having it your way." Eve believed him, and so do we. After all, if we didn't think there was some joy to be had from sinning, why would we choose to sin? No doubt that's why an advice columnist for *Self* magazine suggests, "An affair can help you survive a disappointing marriage and occasionally it gives a woman the energy . . . necessary to leave a bad one."[1]

There is a sense in which Satan is right about the "positive" results of sin. According to Hebrews 11:25, sin does bring pleasure — for a short time. Ultimately, however, sin exacts a devastating toll. *There are no exceptions.*

I have a friend who keeps in his billfold a list of the consequences of sin—such consequences as these:

- Sin steals joy (Psalm 51:12).
- Sin removes confidence (1 John 3:19–21).
- Sin brings guilt (Psalm 51:3).
- Sin gives Satan the upper hand (2 Corinthians 2:9–11).
- Sin quenches God's Spirit (1 Thessalonians 5:19).
- Sin brings physical damage (Psalms 38:1–11; 31:10).
- Sin causes an ache in the soul (Psalm 32:3–4).
- Sin breaks God's heart (Ephesians 4:30).
- Sin opens the door to other sins (Isaiah 30:1).
- Sin breaks fellowship with God (Isaiah 59:1–2).
- Sin produces fear (Proverbs 28:1).
- Sin makes me its slave (John 8:34; Romans 6:16).

When he is tempted to disobey God in some matter, my friend pulls out that list and reads it. He asks himself, "Is this a price I really want to pay? Is this a price I can afford to pay?"

Sometimes, the consequences of our sin are not seen until months or years down the road; sometimes, they don't show up until the next generation; some consequences will be delayed until we stand before God at the judgment seat. That is why we persist in foolishly thinking we have somehow managed to get away with our sin. As we read in Ecclesiastes, "When the sentence for a crime is not quickly carried out, the hearts of the people are filled with schemes to do wrong" (8:11).

One of God's purposes in delaying divine retribution is to give us time to repent: "He is patient with you, not wanting anyone to perish, but everyone to come to repentance" (2 Peter 3:9). Nonetheless, the day of reckoning will come. And when it does, every child of God will wish with all his heart that he had chosen the pathway of obedience.

After years of toying with sin and enjoying its "pleasures," King Solomon finally (and too late) came to the conviction that

> although a wicked man commits a hundred crimes
> and still lives a long time, I know that it will go better
> with God-fearing men, who are reverent before God. . . .
> Here is the conclusion of the matter: Fear God and keep
> his commandments. . . . For God will bring every deed
> into judgment, including every hidden thing.

Ecclesiastes 8:12; 12:13–14

14. "MY SIN ISN'T REALLY THAT BAD."

This lie and the next one—"God can't forgive what I have done" —are two opposite ends of the spectrum. If the Enemy can't get us to believe one, he will get us to believe the other. Both are equally deceptive and both lead to bondage.

Those of us who have grown up in good homes or in the church and have learned how to "act right" are particularly susceptible to this deception. Some of us would never think of being a prostitute or having an abortion or living a homosexual lifestyle. We wouldn't consider using profanity or embezzling money from our employer or divorcing our mate.

Compared to others who commit these kinds of "serious" sins, it's easy for us to feel that we aren't so bad. Our sins of wasting time, self-protection, talking too much, eating or drinking too much, a sharp tongue, a critical spirit, overspending, fear, worry, selfish motives, or complaining don't seem all that major. We may not even consider them to be sins at all—preferring to think of them as weaknesses, struggles, or personality traits.

Eve easily could have viewed her sin this way. After all, she didn't leave her husband; she didn't curse God or deny His existence. All she did, when you think about it, was to take one bite of something God told her not to eat. What was the big deal? The big deal was that God said "Don't," and Eve said "I will."

That one, simple act of eating something God said was off-limits produced enormous consequences—in her body; her mind, will, and emotions; her relationship with God; and her marriage. That one "little" sin influenced her husband to sin, which resulted in the entire human race being plunged into sin. Like a rock thrown into a pond, the ripples caused by sin go on and on.

If only we could see that every single sin is a big deal, that every sin is an act of rebellion and cosmic treason, that every time we choose our way instead of God's way, we are revolting against the God and King of the universe.

As John Bunyan put it, "One leak will sink a ship; and one sin will destroy a sinner."

Or as Bunyan's contemporary, Jeremy Taylor, said, "No sin is small. No grain of sand is small in the mechanism of a watch."

I live in a house with white siding—at least it looks white most of the year. However, when the snow falls in the winter, all of a sudden my house looks dingy and yellow. What may look "clean" when we compare ourselves to other sinners takes on a whole different cast when seen next to the perfect holiness of God.

The way to see the Truth about sin is to see it in the light of who God is. When we gaze upon the brilliance of His untarnished holiness, we become acutely aware of the hideousness of our sin.

The Puritans of the seventeenth and eighteenth centuries were known for their commitment to holiness and obedience. From all outward appearances, there is little for which they could be faulted. Most people do not think of them as great sinners. But as you read their writings, you discover that *they* thought of themselves as great sinners. Because they walked in close communion with God, they cultivated a sense of the horror of their sin, no matter how insignificant it might seem to others. This perspective comes out in the kind of prayers they prayed:

> Unmask to me sin's deformity,
>   that I may hate it, abhor it, flee from it . . .
> Let me never forget that the heinousness of sin
>   lies not so much in the nature of the sin committed,
>   as in the greatness of the person sinned against.[2]

15. "GOD CAN'T FORGIVE WHAT I HAVE DONE."

Whenever I speak on the subject of forgiveness, invariably someone will tell me, "I've never been able to forgive myself for what I've done." Interestingly, the Bible never speaks of the need to forgive ourselves. But I think what many of these women are really saying is that they have never been able to *feel* forgiven for what they have done. They are still carrying a sense of guilt and shame over their failure.

Though they *know* that God can forgive them, deep down they do not *believe* they are truly, fully forgiven. They find it difficult to accept God's mercy and forgiveness. They feel that in order to be restored into favor and fellowship with God there is something further they must do to atone for their sin; that they must do "penance"; that perhaps they can be good enough to make up for the wrong they have done.

The problem is that a lifetime of "good deeds" is not sufficient to deal with the guilt of even one sin against a holy God. Like a stubborn stain that no dry cleaner can remove, sin makes a stain that cannot be washed away by any amount of human effort. There is only one "solution" that can deal with the guilt of our sin:

> What can wash away my sin? Nothing but the blood of Jesus;
> What can make me whole again? Nothing but the blood of Jesus.
>
> Nothing can for sin atone, Nothing but the blood of Jesus;
> Naught of good that I have done, Nothing but the blood of Jesus.[3]

"My sin isn't really that bad," and "God can't forgive what I have done"—the Truth about both of these lies is revealed at Calvary. In Psalm 85.10 (KJV), we find a beautiful description of the Lord Jesus and what He did for us on the cross: "Mercy and truth are met together; righteousness and peace have kissed each other."

It was at Calvary that God's mercy and love for sinners and the Truth of His holy hatred for sin found a meeting place. At Calvary, God heaped upon Jesus all the punishment for all the sin of the world. At the same time, He offered peace and reconciliation to sinners who had been estranged from Him. The Cross shows us in the starkest possible terms what God thinks of our sin; it reveals the incredible cost He paid to redeem us from those "weaknesses" that we trivialize in our minds. The Cross also displays in brilliant Technicolor the love and mercy of God for even the "chief of sinners."

William Cowper was one of the finest English writers of the nineteenth century. But he carried significant emotional baggage and turmoil into his adult years. As a young man, he experienced a mental breakdown, attempted suicide, and was placed in an insane asylum for eighteen months. It was during this confinement that he read a verse of Scripture that changed his life. He discovered that Jesus Christ "is set forth to be a propitiation through faith in his blood, to declare his righteousness for the remission of sins that are past, through the forbearance of God" (Romans 3:25 KJV).

Once he saw the Truth and embraced it, Cowper entered into a personal relationship with Christ and was granted the knowledge that his sins had been forgiven. Years later, he expressed the wonder of that forgiveness in a hymn that has brought hope to repentant sinners for more than two hundred years. Though you may have sung them many times before, stop and sing these words once again—slowly, as if you had never heard them before—and rest and rejoice in God's redeeming mercy and love:

> There is a fountain filled with blood
> Drawn from Immanuel's veins,
> And sinners plunged beneath that flood
> Lose all their guilty stains.
>
> The dying thief rejoiced to see
> That fountain in his day,
> And there may I, though vile as he,
> Wash all my sins away.
>
> Dear dying Lamb, Thy precious blood
> Shall never lose its pow'r,
> Till all the ransomed Church of God
> Be saved to sin no more.

16. "I AM NOT FULLY RESPONSIBLE FOR MY ACTIONS AND REACTIONS."

Anna Russell's "Psychiatric Folksong" expresses our natural tendency to blame others for our behavior:

At three I had a feeling of ambivalence toward my brothers,
And so it follows naturally I poisoned all my lovers.
But I am happy; now I've learned the lesson this has taught;
That everything I do that's wrong is someone else's fault.

If we go back to the Garden of Eden, it becomes apparent that this is one of the oldest forms of deception.

After Adam and Eve ate the forbidden fruit, God came to hold them accountable for what they had done. (This is a recurring theme throughout the Scripture—we will give account to God for every deed we have done.) Notice that God did not approach them as a family unit. He didn't ask: "What have you [plural] done?" Neither did He ask Adam and Eve to explain each other's behavior. He didn't ask Adam, "What did Eve do?"; nor did He ask Eve, "What did your husband do?" He approached first Adam, then Eve, and asked each one individually, "What have *you* [singular] done?"

God's question to Adam was pointed and specific: "Have *you* eaten from the tree that I commanded you not to eat from?" (Genesis 3:11, italics added). Likewise, God asked Eve, "What is this *you* have done?" (v. 13, italics added). God was asking for a simple admission of the Truth.

As the account unfolds, we see that Adam and Eve both chose to play "The Blame Game" rather than take personal responsibility for their actions. "Have you eaten from the tree?" God inquired of Adam. Adam's answer: "The woman you put here with me—she gave me some fruit from the tree, and I ate it" (v. 12).

"Eve, what have *you* done?" Answer: "The serpent deceived me, and I ate" (v. 13).

In both cases, their response was accurate. Eve *was* the woman God had given to Adam. And she *had* given the fruit to her husband. The Serpent *had,* in fact, deceived Eve. However, by shifting the blame to another, Adam and Eve were attempting to diminish their own responsibility in the matter.

God was not asking them what someone else had done to make them sin; He was asking them to take responsibility for their own behavior. Regardless of what had influenced them to make that choice, it was still their choice.

Adam and Eve may have been the first, but they certainly weren't the last in what has become a long, unbroken line of "blame-shifters."

The "game" that began in the Garden is one we have all played. In fact, we are naturally experts at it, as illustrated by these testimonies:

By constantly blaming others, blaming circumstances, and blaming God, *I found myself totally irresponsible for my life, my sins, and my choices—and then I was trapped and felt helpless and out of control.*

I used to believe I was easily depressed due to being a victim. I felt like being depressed was not *my fault. When I began to realize that depression was caused by my choice to be angry, I began to take responsibility for my sin and found freedom.*

I had an ungodly relationship with a male coworker. I relied on him for emotional support and affection because my husband was keeping secrets from me, using pornography, and not "being there" for me. In my eyes, my husband's behavior had pushed me into this relationship. *I was giving myself a reason and an excuse that "it was not as bad as what he was doing."*

When we are angry, depressed, bitter, annoyed, impatient, or fearful, our natural response is to shift at least some of the responsibility onto the people or circumstances that "made" us that way.

I have listened to perhaps hundreds of women tell me about their broken marriages. Invariably, they describe their ex-mate's offenses that destroyed the marriage. Offhand, I cannot recall a single instance in which a woman said, "I contributed to the breakup of my marriage through my wrong attitudes and responses," or "I was wrong to divorce my husband."

Countless women have explained to me the circumstances that "caused" their indebtedness, their eating disorder, their immorality, or their estranged relationship with their parents. Only rarely do I hear women take personal responsibility for their own choices that have created these issues in their lives.

I will never forget the day a middle-aged woman came to the platform to give a testimony during one of our women's revival conferences. She introduced herself by saying that she had been a therapist for twenty-two years. Her next words were to the point and deeply penetrating. Brokenly, she said, "I want to repent before You, my God, and before you, my sisters, for leading you astray and for telling you lies— for not saying, 'You are solely and personally responsible for your own behavior, no matter what anyone else does.' I'm sorry!"

The Enemy tells us that if we accept full responsibility for our own choices, we will be plagued with unnecessary guilt.

The Truth is that only by accepting full responsibility for our actions and attitudes can we ever be fully free from guilt. As one writer said:

> Sin is the best news there is, the best news there could be in our predicament.
>
> Because with sin, there's a way out. There's the possibility of repentance. You can't repent of confusion or psychological flaws inflicted by your parents—you're stuck with them. But you can repent of sin. Sin and repentance are the only grounds for hope and joy.[4]

🍎 17. "I CANNOT WALK IN CONSISTENT VICTORY OVER SIN."

Anyone who has been a Christian for any length of time can probably relate to the frustration expressed by "Heather":

⁂

There are so many sins that control my life. How will I ever be free? I feel like I am a hopeless case. I want so badly to get rid of these sins, but they continue to rule my flesh. I feel embarrassed to come to God with these things over and over again. When I pile them all together, it seems even more hopeless. How do I stay free from this lie? I want to be changed.

⁂

These words remind me of the heart-cry of the apostle Paul:

I find this law at work: When I want to do good,
evil is right there with me. For in my inner being
I delight in God's law; but I see another law at work
in the members of my body, waging war against the law
of my mind and making me a prisoner of the law of sin at
work within my members. What a wretched man I am!
Who will rescue me from this body of death?

Romans 7:21–24

More than half of the women we surveyed acknowledged that they had bought into the lie that they could not live in consistent victory over sin. It is easy to see how Satan uses this lie to place believers in bondage.

As we see in the passage above, any person who is a true child of God has been given a new nature—a nature that desires to obey God. Deep down, every true believer *wants* to live a life that is pleasing to God. (The person who does not have any such desire should question whether he has ever been truly converted.)

However, according to the Scripture, even after we are born again, our "flesh" (our natural inclinations) continues to wage war against the Spirit of God living within us.

The Spirit says: Forgive.
The flesh says: Hold a grudge.

The Spirit says: Be temperate.
The flesh says: Eat whatever you want, whenever you feel like it.

The Spirit says: Give that money to someone in need.
The flesh says: Spend that money on yourself.

The Spirit says: Spend some time in the Word and prayer.
The flesh says: You've had a long day; chill out in front of the TV for the evening.

The Spirit says: Hold your tongue. What you are about to say is not kind or necessary.
The flesh says: Tell it like it is!

Every time we choose to give in to the flesh, rather than yielding to the Spirit of God, we allow sin to gain mastery over us. On the other hand, every time we say yes to the Spirit, we give Him greater control of our lives.

When we make repeated choices to obey sin rather than God, we establish habit patterns that are extremely difficult to break—we choose to live as sin's slaves. For a while, we may find ourselves trying to do right, then failing, trying and failing, trying and failing. That is when the devil begins to convince us that it can never be any different, that we will always be enslaved to that sinful habit. We think, *What's the use? I'm just going to blow it again! I'm going to be defeated by this for the rest of my life.* So we give up. What has happened? Satan has succeeded in making us believe we cannot walk in consistent victory over temptation and sin. Though the specific issues varied, that is exactly what happened to "Christine" and "Cheryl":

I struggled with being emotionally attracted to women in a way that I clearly knew was wrong. As hard as I fought within myself, my thoughts just got worse and worse. I didn't think I could control my thoughts. *I knew I wasn't pure before God, but I couldn't seem to clean myself up.*

I have been in bondage to food for years. I struggle with it every day. I constantly feel *like it is beyond me to change it and that* I will never be victorious. *I might do well for a while, but the lies creep back in and destroy me.*

Remember that what we believe determines the way we live. If *we believe* we are going to sin, then *we will.* If *we believe* we have to live in bondage, then *we will.* If *we believe* that we can't live victorious lives, *we won't.*

"Cheryl" does have one thing right, though. She believes that "it is beyond me to change it." Strange as it may seem, that realization is actually a major step toward experiencing victory over sin.

The Truth is, you and I are powerless to change ourselves, for "Apart from me," Jesus said, "you can do nothing" (John 15:5).

So what are we to do? How can we be set free from habitual sin? It is the Truth that sets us free.

The Truth is, through Christ's finished work on the cross, we can live in victory over sin; Satan is no longer our master, and we no longer have to live as slaves to sin. If you are in Christ, the Truth is:

> You have been set free from sin and have become slaves to
> righteousness.... Through Christ Jesus the law of the
> Spirit of life set me free from the law of sin and death.

Romans 6:18; 8:2

GOOD NEWS FOR SINNERS

As we have seen, Satan promised Eve that if she would eat the forbidden fruit, her eyes would be opened, she would be like God, and she would know good and evil.

The Truth is, the moment she ate,

- she became spiritually blind, unable to see the Truth;
- though she had been created in the likeness of God, that image was shattered, and she took on a sinful nature, as unlike God as darkness is the opposite of light;
- she did gain the knowledge of evil (something God never intended), but fellowship with God was broken, and she became incapable of being righteous.

Likewise, every man, woman, and child who has ever lived since that day has been born into that same fallen condition: spiritually blind, a sinner, separated from God, and incapable of doing anything to please Him. Because of our sin, we are all under the righteous judgment of God.

The Good News—the Gospel—is that Jesus came to this earth and took upon Himself the penalty for all of Eve's sin and ours, so the devastating consequences of that sin could be reversed. Through His sinless life, His death on Calvary as the sinner's substitute, and His victorious resurrection, we can be fully forgiven for all our sin, we can be reconciled to the God we have offended, and we can have the power to live holy lives.

We do not receive this forgiveness and this right standing before a holy God by being born into a Christian home, growing up in the church, being baptized or confirmed, doing good deeds, going forward during an altar call, having an emotional experience, reciting a prayer, or being active in church. We are not saved from sin by trusting in anything that we have done. The only means of eternal salvation is through placing our trust in what Jesus did for us on the cross, when He died in our place.

I often receive notes from women who are wrestling with doubts about their salvation. Some of these women know all the "right answers," but they are still plagued with guilt over the "sin issue" in their lives. In many cases, I believe that is because they have never truly repented of their sin and placed their faith in Christ alone to save them. They may be religious, but they have never been made righteous.

What about you, my friend? The Enemy wants to keep you in bondage to fear, doubt, and guilt. God wants you to walk in freedom, faith, and assurance of forgiveness. No matter how "good" you may be, the only way you can ever be made right with God is through faith in Christ. And no matter how "great" a sinner you may have been, His grace is sufficient for you. Through the death of Christ, God has made the only acceptable provision for your sin.

If you have never dealt with the issue of your sin in this way, if you do not know that you are a child of God, I want to appeal to you to stop and get it settled before moving on to the next chapter. Don't let the Enemy blind you or hold you hostage any longer. Your eternal destiny is at stake.

Acknowledge to God that you have sinned against His law and that you cannot save yourself. Thank Him for sending Jesus to take the penalty that you deserve by dying for your sin. By faith, believe on Christ to save you, and receive His free gift of life. Tell God that you want to turn away from your sin, to place all your trust in Christ alone, and to let Him be the Lord of your life. Now, thank Him for forgiving your sin; thank Him for the gift of His Spirit, who has come to live in you and who will enable you to walk in victory over sin, as you yield to Him. (If you have just placed your faith in Christ, I would encourage you to turn to page 275, where I have recommended some resources to help you grow in your new life.)

Whether you have just become a child of God, or you have known the Lord for some time, in light of where God found us and what He has done for us, let us pray with the Puritans of old:

Grant me never to lose sight of
    the exceeding sinfulness of sin,
    the exceeding righteousness of salvation,
    the exceeding glory of Christ,
    the exceeding beauty of holiness,
    the exceeding wonder of grace.[5]

THE LIE	THE TRUTH
13. I CAN SIN AND GET AWAY WITH IT.	• The choices I make today will have consequences; I will reap what I sow. • Sin's pleasures only last for a season. • Sin exacts a devastating toll. There are no exceptions. • If I play with fire, I will get burned. I will not escape the consequences of my sin.
14. MY SIN ISN'T REALLY THAT BAD.	• Every act of sin is an act of rebellion against God. • No sin is small.
15. GOD CAN'T FORGIVE WHAT I HAVE DONE.	• The blood of Jesus is sufficient to cover any and every sin I have committed. • There is no sin too great for God to forgive. • God's grace is greater than the greatest sin anyone could ever commit.
16. I AM NOT FULLY RESPONSIBLE FOR MY ACTIONS AND REACTIONS.	• God does not hold me accountable for the actions of others. • I am responsible for my own choices.
17. I CANNOT WALK IN CONSISTENT VICTORY OVER SIN.	• If I am a child of God, I don't have to sin. • I am not a slave to sin. Through Christ, I have been set free from sin. • By God's grace and through the finished work of Christ on the cross, I can experience victory over sin.

1. AGREE with God.

What lies have you believed about sin?

_____

_____

2. ACCEPT responsibility.

How has believing those lies manifested itself in the way you live (e.g., attitudes, actions)?

_____

_____

3. AFFIRM the Truth.

Read aloud each of the Truths listed on page 112. Which of these Truths do you particularly need to embrace at this time?

_____

Renew your mind (your thinking) by the Word of God. Read the following passages aloud. What do these verses reveal about the nature of sin, its effects in our lives, and God's provision for our sin?

Psalm 32:1–5

_____

James 1:13–15

_____

1 John 1:5–9

_____

Romans 6:11–14

_____

4. ACT on the Truth.

What specific step(s) of action do you need to take to align your life with the Truth you have seen about sin?

_____

_____

5. ASK God to help you walk in the Truth.

Holy, holy God, I confess that I have often trivialized sin and its consequences. I realize that all sin is rebellion against You and grieves Your heart. Thank You for the blood of Jesus that has satisfied Your wrath against my sin. Thank You, Lord Jesus, for taking on Yourself all the guilt and penalty for my sin, and crediting to my account all the righteousness of God. Please forgive me for not taking seriously enough what it cost You to deal with my sin. Thank You for the blessing of full forgiveness and that I can stand before You, free from all guilt and condemnation. Thank You that through the power of the Cross and the indwelling Holy Spirit, I don't have to live in bondage to sin any longer, but have been set free to obey You. I praise You for Your promise that one day You will deliver Your children from even the presence of sin and will take us to heaven to live with You forever. In Jesus' name. Amen.

CHAPTER FIVE

LIES WOMEN BELIEVE... ABOUT PRIORITIES

Dear diary,

Whew! Life has been a whirlwind. It's been months since I've had a chance to sit down and put my thoughts on paper. We hardly have time to breathe these days. The boys are so active; I feel like I spend all my time chasing them around and picking up after them. It's amazing how fast they can make a mess! They are growing up so quickly—they'll be gone before we know it. I don't want to miss out on the opportunity, while they are still young, to play together, to enjoy being together, and to teach them the things that really matter in life.

It's harvesttime, which is always the busiest time of year for Adam. We don't get to see a lot of each other these days. I wish we had more time to just sit and talk—about us, about the children, about our future.

With all the activity around here, I haven't had much time to

take walks and talk with God like I used to do. Things were a lot
simpler before we had kids. There just aren't enough hours in each
day. I fall into bed exhausted at night, and get up and go through
the same routine the next day . . . and the next . . . and the next . . .

We have looked at what I believe are the three most fundamental and universal areas of deception: what we believe about God, what we believe about ourselves, and what we believe about sin. To a large measure, these determine what we believe about everything else. If we have been deceived in these areas, there is a far greater chance of our being deceived in other matters.

In the next several chapters, we want to examine a number of practical areas where many Christian women have been deceived, beginning with the matter of our priorities. A placard I saw hanging in a women's boutique some years ago reveals something of the fruit of that deception:

I am woman.
I am invincible.
I am tired.

The expression, borrowed from Helen Reddy's Grammy-winning song of the early 1970s, was undoubtedly intended to evoke a smile. But it also captures something of the struggle in every woman's life to know how to juggle the many demands and responsibilities that come with each season of life.

Most of the women I know do not feel invincible—to the contrary, many of them battle feelings of inadequacy and insecurity. But most of the women I know are tired. They often feel incapable of managing the many hats they wear and balancing the various responsibilities they carry.

Those frustrations are fueled by a number of lies the Enemy has planted in our collective and personal thinking. Lies such as . . .

🍎 18. "I DON'T HAVE TIME TO DO EVERY- THING I'M SUPPOSED TO DO."

By a long shot, this was the number one lie the women we sur- veyed identified with. Seventy percent of the women said they had found themselves believing this lie. I wasn't surprised by those results.

After all, if you ask a woman today, "How are you doing?" chances are the response will be a sigh or a groan, followed by words some- thing like:

- "I'm so busy!"
- "We've got so much going on in our family!"
- "I just can't keep up with everything I've got to do!"
- "I'm exhausted!"

More often than not, I find that women (and Christian women are no exception) feel overwhelmed by how much they have to do and how little time they have to do it. As a result, many women are living breathless, frazzled, discouraged lives.

Years ago, I read that the average woman today has the equiva- lent of *fifty* full-time servants, in the form of modern, timesaving devices and equipment. That figure may or may not be accurate, but we certainly have many conveniences available to us that were un- known to women of past generations. Imagine going back to the days when there were no dishwashers, microwaves, washing machines, dry- ers, or automobiles—or even further back to a time when people had never heard of indoor plumbing or electricity.

I remember as a child going through an exhibit at the World's Fair that attempted to envision "the lifestyle of the future." Hi-tech and electronic gadgets performed all kinds of household chores and daily tasks, leaving people free to sit back and relax or to use their time for more "important" things. Well, the future is here. We have devices and gadgets that even the most imaginative minds never dreamed of when I was a little girl. So why are our lives more harried and hur- ried than ever? Why are we so stressed out?

There are probably a number of explanations. However, one reason is that we have accepted the lie that we don't have time to do everything we are supposed to do.

The fact is, we have no more or less time than any other human being who has ever lived. No one, regardless of his position or responsibilities, has ever had more than 24 hours in a day, 168 hours in a week, 52 weeks in a year.

In fact, the Lord Jesus Himself was given only a few short years on earth to accomplish the entire plan of redemption. Talk about a long "to do" list! Yet, at the end of His life, Jesus was able to lift His eyes to His Father and say, "I have glorified thee on the earth: I have *finished the work* which thou gavest me to do" (John 17:4 KJV, italics added).

I find that truly amazing. Rarely can I say at the end of the day that I have completed the work I set out to do that day. To the contrary, I frequently drop into bed at night with a long, mental list of the unfinished tasks I had hoped to take care of that day. How was it possible for Jesus to finish His life's work—especially in such a short period of time?

In Jesus' words, we find a clue—a powerful Truth that sets us free from the bondage of hurry and frustration about all we have to do. Notice what work Jesus completed in the thirty-three years He was here on the earth: "I have finished the work *which thou gavest me to do.*" That is the secret. Jesus didn't finish everything His disciples wanted Him to do. (Some of them were hoping He would overthrow the Roman government!) He didn't finish everything the multitudes wanted Him to do. (There were still people who were sick and lonely and dying.) But He did finish the work that *God* gave Him to do.

There is virtually never time in a twenty-four-hour day for me to do everything that is on everyone else's "to do" list for me. There is seldom time to do everything that is on my own "to do" list. I cannot meet with every person who wants an appointment, call every person who wants to talk, counsel with every person who has a need, tackle every project that people think I would be good at, read all the books I'd like to read, spend the kind of time I'd like to spend with my friends, and keep every room in my house presentable for guests who drop in. It's just not physically possible.

What a relief to realize *I don't have to do all those things!*

The Truth is that all I have to do is the work God assigns to me. What a freedom it has been for me to accept that *there is time for me to do everything that is on God's "to do" list for my day, for my week, and for my life!*

The frustration comes when I attempt to take on responsibilities that are not on His agenda for me. When I establish my own agenda or let others determine the priorities for my life, rather than taking time to discern what it is that God wants me to do, I end up buried under piles of half-finished, poorly done, or never-attempted projects and tasks. I live with guilt, frustration, and haste, rather than enjoying the peaceful, well-ordered life that He intends.

It is important to keep in mind that God's "to do" list for my life is not the same as His list for anyone else's life. Jesus said, "I have finished the work which thou gavest *me* to do"—not "the work which you gave Peter or John or My mother to do." The work God has for me to do is not the same as what He has for you or for my friends or coworkers. What God has called you to do as a mother with three toddlers will not be the same as the "job description" He has for your husband, or for a single, young woman or an empty nester.

Further, there are different seasons of our lives, and God's assignments for me in my forties will not be exactly the same as what He gave me to do as a teenager or what He will have in mind for me as an elderly woman.

By the way, there is another, related lie that women in our generation have bought into. In a sense, it is the opposite of the lie that we don't have enough time to do everything we're "supposed" to do. It is the lie that *"I can do it all"*—that "I should be able to be an ideal wife and mother, keep my house clean and organized, prepare healthy meals for my family, be active in my kids' school and my church and community, stay physically fit, keep up on current events, *and* have a full-time job outside my home."

Women who subconsciously believe they are supposed to be able to juggle all these roles are likely to end up exhausted and overwhelmed by all the demands on their time.

The Truth is, no woman can wear all those hats effectively. Sooner or later, something (or someone) is going to suffer.

Frustration is the by-product of attempting to fulfill responsibilities God does not intend for us to carry. Freedom, joy, and fruitfulness come from seeking to determine God's priorities for each season of life, and then setting out to fulfill those priorities, in the power of His Spirit, realizing that He has provided the necessary time and ability to do *everything* that *He* has called us to do.

The following testimonies illustrate how Satan's lies about priorities and time put us in bondage and how the Truth has the power to set us free:

I felt guilty for not being able to help all those "good Christian" causes. I never felt that I was succeeding or doing anything well. What a relief it has been to learn that "there is enough time to do everything that God wants me to do." On many days, when I feel myself getting stressed, I repeat that Truth over and over again. Just speaking the Truth helps to calm me. Now the days don't seem to fly by so fast, and I can truly live "in the moment," not "by the clock."

I have believed the lie that I don't have time to get everything done. I have not been meeting my responsibilities adequately, and I have experienced a desperate, hopeless feeling because my home is always messy and my children are behaving poorly.

Once I realized that I have enough time to do what God has given me to do, then I had to admit that I was attempting to do things He has not assigned to me. I am starting the process of removing things from my life as I discover what doesn't belong and finding things I can delegate. I am also learning to communicate with my husband so he can release me from things he doesn't care about and be clear about what he does care about. This is not an easy process, but I have simplified a few things so far, and I hope to gain momentum as I continue, until my life is under control and I am free to do that which God has given me. This is only happening with the guidance and grace of the Lord.

I believed it was my duty to serve whenever the church needed me. If I saw something that needed to be done, I had to do it. As a result, I was overextended—doing something at church almost every day of the week. I was doing everything because I "had" to, not because I wanted to. I couldn't get anyone to help because I would not ask anyone to work at any job as hard as I did. I felt I was the "only one" who could do all the things I did.

After I finally burned out, my pastor was able to help me see that I did not have to do everything—only the things the Father gave me to do. I continue to do some activities, but only those that I know are what God wants me to do. I have learned to say no when I know it is not something God is calling me to do.

None of the things I was doing was bad—they just weren't what God would have me do. By doing them I was squeezing out the things He was calling me to do and be. God set me free from the bondage of busyness to allow me to truly be His servant. I no longer look for serving opportunities but look to God as His servant, ready to go wherever He wills.

19. "I CAN MAKE IT WITHOUT CONSISTENT TIME IN THE WORD AND PRAYER."

Unlike the lie we have just considered, few Christian women could bring themselves to say this lie aloud. Yet nearly 48 percent of the women who completed our survey admitted that they have believed this lie. In fact, this particular lie ranked number four in frequency.

The essence of Satan's deception is that we can live our lives independently of God. The Enemy doesn't care if we "believe" in God, if we are doctrinally orthodox, or if we fill our schedules with a lot of "spiritual activities," as long as he can get us to run on our own steam, rather than living in conscious dependence upon the power of the Holy Spirit.

If he can get us to try to "live the Christian life" without cultivating an intimate relationship with the Lord Jesus, he knows we will be spiritually impotent and defeated. If he can get us to do a great many things "for God" without consciously seeking the will of God through His Word and prayer, we may stir up a lot of religious dust, but we won't do Satan's kingdom any real damage. If he can get us to operate on our own thoughts and ideas, rather than seeking the wisdom that comes from God, he knows we will eventually get sucked into the world's destructive way of thinking.

"Yvette" shared the practical impact that this lie has had in her life:

When I spend time in the Word and prayer, my daily life seems to flow along smoothly—even with three children under the age of five. But then I get complacent and think what a wonder woman I am and stop making it a priority. Before I know it, my life is in chaos. I am screaming at my kids and on the verge of child abuse, trying to figure out how I ended up like this. And what can I do to fix it? Unfortunately, it takes me a while to realize I can't—that I need God! The lies of Satan creep in so subtly, and if I'm not in the Word, I start believing them.

Satan knows that if he succeeds in getting us to live independently of the Word of God, we become more vulnerable to deception in every area of our lives. Six times in the Old Testament we are told that David "inquired of the LORD" (1 Samuel 23:2, 4; 30:8; 2 Samuel 2:1; 5:19, 23). He knew he was nothing apart from God—that he could not make it without the Lord. In fact, the first thing he did every morning—before turning to the business of the day—was to turn his heart toward the Lord in prayer:

My voice shalt thou hear in the morning, O LORD;
in the morning will I direct my prayer
unto thee, and will look up.

I rise before dawn and cry for help;
I have put my hope in your word.

Psalms 5:3 KJV; 119:147

I know the great value and importance of spending time alone with God in His Word and prayer each day—I've even written a book on the subject. But far too often I find myself turning my attention to the details and tasks of the day without first taking adequate time to "inquire of the Lord."

When I do so, what I am really saying (though I'd never actually *say* it) is that I can handle that day on my own—apart from the presence, wisdom, and grace of God. I am saying I can do my work, keep my home, handle my relationships, and deal with my circumstances without Him. That independent, self-sufficient spirit is an expression of pride. The Scripture teaches, "God resists the proud" (James 4:6 NKJV). If I walk in pride, I must be prepared for God to resist me and my efforts.

Sometimes I get the sense that God may be saying to me, "You want to handle this day by yourself? Go ahead." The result? At best, an empty, fruitless day lived by and for myself. At worst, oh, what a mess I end up making of things.

On the other hand, "God gives grace to the humble." When I start the day by humbling myself and acknowledging that I can't make it on my own—that I *need* Him—I can count on His divine enabling to carry me through the day.

The Truth is, *apart from "abiding in Him"*—living in constant, conscious union with and dependence on Him—*I cannot do anything of spiritual or eternal value.* Oh, I can create a lot of activity, I can make a lot of decisions, but I will end up having nothing of real value to show for my life.

The Truth is, *it is impossible for me to be the woman He wants me to be apart from my spending consistent time cultivating a relationship with Him, in the Word and prayer.*

20. "A CAREER OUTSIDE THE HOME IS MORE VALUABLE AND FULFILLING THAN BEING A WIFE AND MOTHER."

Half a century ago, a handful of determined women set out to achieve a philosophical and cultural revolution. Convinced that women needed to throw off the shackles of male oppression, they wrote books, published articles, taught college courses, marched in the streets, lobbied Congress, and in myriad ways succeeded in capturing the minds and hearts of millions of women.

They redefined what it means to be a woman and tossed out widely held views of a woman's priorities and mission in life. Concepts such as *virtue, chastity, discretion, domesticity, submission,* and *modesty* were largely eliminated from our vocabulary, and replaced with *choice, divorce, infidelity,* and *unisex lifestyles.* The daughters and granddaughters of that generation have never known any other way of thinking.

One of the most devastating objectives and effects of this "new" view of womanhood has been to demean marriage and motherhood and to move women—both physically and emotionally—out of their homes and into the workforce. Dr. Dorothy Patterson observes:

Women have been liberated right out of the genuine freedom they enjoyed for centuries to oversee the home, rear the children, and pursue personal creativity; they have been brainwashed to believe that the

absence of a titled, payroll occupation enslaves a woman to failure, bore-
dom, and imprisonment within the confines of home.[1]

Statistics indicate that the gender gap has narrowed dramatically in
matters of hiring practices, pay scales, and educational opportunities
—results that activists have worked long and hard to achieve. But what
about the unintended consequences of this newfound freedom? Whoever expected we would have to live with such things as . . .

- pressure placed on women by their peers to "do more" than
  be "just a wife and mother";
- the status of a "homemaker" being devalued to something less
  than that of a serf;
- millions of infants and toddlers being dropped off at day care
  centers before daylight and picked up after dark;
- millions of children coming home from school to empty
  houses or being relegated to after-school child care programs;
- mothers giving their best energy and time to persons other
  than their husbands and children, leaving those women per-
  petually exhausted and edgy;
- families that seldom sit down and have a meal together;
- children subsisting on frozen dinners and fast food eaten on
  the run;
- emotional and physical affairs being fanned by married
  women spending more quality time with men at work than
  they do with their own husbands;
- women gaining enough financial independence to free them
  to leave their husbands;
- women being exposed day after day to coarse language and
  behavior and sexual innuendos in the workplace;
- women who don't have the time or energy to cultivate a
  close relationship with their children and who end up permanently estranged from their grown children;

- children spending countless hours being entertained by videos, TV, electronic games, and computers;
- inadequately supervised children becoming exposed to and lured into pornography, alcohol, drugs, sex, and violence;
- elderly parents having to be placed in institutions because their daughters and daughters-in-law are working full-time and can't manage their care.

In determining our priorities as Christian women, we must first ask: Why did God make women? What is His purpose and mission for our lives? The Word of God provides women of every generation and culture with the Truth about our created purpose and primary role and calling. When we embrace the Truth and establish our priorities and schedules around it, we experience true liberation.

In Genesis 2:18 we find the first and clearest statement of why God created the woman:

The LORD God said, "It is not good for the man to be alone. I will make a helper suitable for him."

There you have it—God created the woman to be a helper to the man—to complete him, to be suited to his needs. Her life was to center on his, not his on hers. She was made from the man, made for the man, and given as God's gift to the man. Her relationship with her husband was the first and primary sphere in which she was to move and serve. Her husband was responsible to work to provide for their material needs. She was to be his helper and companion in reflecting the image of God, taking dominion over the earth, and reproducing a godly seed.

Together, they were to populate the earth with future generations of men and women who would love God and seek to fulfill His purposes in the world. The woman was uniquely designed and equipped —physiologically, emotionally, mentally, and spiritually—by her Creator to be a bearer and nurturer of life. In a multitude of ways, she was endowed with the ability to add life, beauty, richness, fullness, grace, and joy to the family unit. There is no greater measure of her worth or success as a woman than the extent to which she serves as the heart of her home.

In his first letter to Timothy, the apostle Paul spelled out several things that had to be true of widows before they were entitled to be cared for by the church. In that list we find a "job description" for godly women in every season of life. Paul honored older women whose lives centered on their homes and who gave themselves to serving and ministering to the needs of others. The qualifications Paul listed ought to be high on every Christian woman's list of priorities:

> No widow may be put on the list of widows unless she . . .
> has been faithful to her husband, and is well known for her
> good deeds, such as bringing up children, showing hospitality,
> washing the feet of the saints, helping those in trouble
> and devoting herself to all kinds of good deeds.

1 Timothy 5:9–10

Paul was obviously addressing women who had been married, in keeping with the biblical perspective that marriage is God's norm for most women. However, according to 1 Corinthians 7:32–35, women who are unmarried are still called to be "homemakers," though in a different sense. They are to devote their energies and efforts to building the household of faith; they are to live selfless lives that revolve not around their own interests and aspirations, but around Christ and His kingdom.

The Scripture is clear that a married woman's life and ministry are to be centered in her home. This is not to suggest that it is necessarily wrong for a wife and mother to have a job outside her home—unless that job in any way competes with or diminishes her effectiveness in fulfilling her primary calling at home. Further, it is important for women to evaluate their reason(s) for working out-side their home and to identify any deception behind those reasons.

For example, it is widely assumed today that a family simply can-not make it without two incomes. It is true that one of the unfortu-nate by-products of the feminist revolution is that our economy has become dependent on two-income families. However, that does not necessarily mean that families cannot survive on one income.

The Truth is that God gave to the man the primary responsibil-ity to be the "breadwinner" for his wife and children. The Enemy has seen to it that it has become extremely difficult to function this way, but it is always possible to live according to the Truth if we want to.

I have a number of close friends with six, seven, eight, and nine children who have chosen for the mother to stay at home with the children. No, it's not easy; they don't have a lot of material things many people consider necessities today. Yes, they make sacrifices—in a sense; but the sacrifices pale beside what they are gaining in exchange. In virtually every case,

- these families are content and have joy;
- they have a better sense about values and the things that really matter than do many two-income families;
- they have learned how to pray and depend on God for every-thing from "daily bread" to college tuition;
- the parents know where their children are and are able to monitor and direct their activities;
- the parents and children have close, loving relationships with each other;
- they are actively involved in serving others in practical ways that many families don't have time (or energy) to do when both parents are working outside the home.

Now you tell me—who is really sacrificing?

Even many secular women recognize the tension that is created when a woman tries to marry a career with a family. In an inter-view, actress Katharine Hepburn said:

> I'm not sure any woman can successfully pursue a career and be a mother at the same time. The trouble with women today is that they want everything. But no one can have it all.[2]

Another actress, Joanne Woodward, agrees:

> My career has suffered because of the children, and my children have suffered because of my career. . . . I've been torn and haven't been able to function fully in either arena. I don't know of one person who does both successfully, and I know a lot of working mothers.[3]

In a fallen world, I realize there are some situations where the "ideal" may not be possible. However, realities such as the preva-lence of divorce and single moms should not make us throw out the ideal. It should make us more conscious of the desirability of God's way. We must resist caving in to the culture. After all, it is the culture of "working moms"—at least in part—that has given rise to an in-creased divorce rate, more single moms, more affairs, more women on welfare, more teen violence, and more stressed- out, depressed, ex-hausted women.

As Dorothy Patterson reminds women,

> It is true that many "perfect jobs" may come and go during the child-rearing years, but only one will absolutely never come along again—the job of rearing your own children and allowing them the increasingly rare opportunity to grow up at home.[4]

INSIGHTS FROM A REFRIGERATOR

My refrigerator serves as a backdrop for photographs of my friends and their families. Mounted in acrylic frames with magnets on the back, the pictures cover almost every square inch of available space. The nearly ninety families represented have a total of some three hundred children (not to mention scores of grandchildren).

Recently I spent a couple of hours in an annual ritual of replacing old photos with new ones that had been sent to me during the Christmas season.

When all the new photos were in place, I sat back to survey the "big picture." I reviewed some of the highlights these families had experienced over the past year. Eight had been blessed with the birth of a new baby. At least seven had a grandchild born. Seven had a son or daughter get married. Fifteen had moved. Six had made or were in the process of making a vocational change.

Nearly all the faces in these photos are smiling. But behind some of the near-perfect poses, I know there is more. Several individuals have confided a burden in relation to the physical or spiritual condition of specific family members. Three have recently buried a member of their immediate family. One couple is in the midst of an ugly divorce.

As I pondered the scene before me, I was struck with the wonder and significance of the family—for better or worse. The family is at the heart of what really matters to all of us. If things aren't well at home, every other area of life is affected. I looked at those scores of women sitting like mother hens surrounded by their brood of young ones, and I felt an enormous sense of gratitude for the willingness of those women to be givers and nurturers of life.

In the middle of all the photos, I have placed a bumper sticker you may recall seeing several years ago: "Life: What a Beautiful Choice." These women have chosen life by bearing children (something only a woman can do, I might add); and they are choosing life every day . . .

- with every meal they prepare;
- with every load of dirty clothes they wash;
- with every trip they make to the grocery store, to school, to the dentist, to piano lessons, to soccer practice, or to the shoe store;

- with every scraped knee they bandage;
- with every encouraging word they speak;
- with every night hour they spend rocking a sick or scared child;
- with every dispute they arbitrate;
- with every moment they spend building Legos, coloring, helping with math problems, reading a Bible story, or listening to a husband or child describe his day;
- with every moment they spend interceding for the spiritual growth and protection of their family.

Day in and day out, they are building a home; they are being life-givers; they are laying a foundation and building a memorial that will outlive them for generations to come; they are honoring their Creator in the greatest possible way.

THE LIE	THE TRUTH
18. I DON'T HAVE TIME TO DO EVERYTHING I'M SUPPOSED TO DO.	• There is time in every day to do everything that *God* wants me to do.
19. I CAN MAKE IT WITHOUT CONSISTENT TIME IN THE WORD AND PRAYER.	• It is impossible for me to be the woman God wants me to be apart from spending consistent time cultivating a relationship with Him in the Word and prayer.
20. A CAREER OUTSIDE THE HOME IS MORE VALUABLE AND FULFILLING THAN BEING A WIFE AND MOTHER.	• In the will of God, there is no higher, holier calling than to be a wife and mother. • God uniquely designed the woman to be a bearer and nurturer of life. • There is no greater measure of a woman's worth or success than the extent to which she serves as the heart of her home. • God's plan is that a woman's primary attention and efforts should be devoted to ministering to the needs of her husband and children.

1. AGREE with God.

What lies have you believed about your priorities?

_____

_____

2. ACCEPT responsibility.

How has believing those lies manifested itself in the way you live (e.g., attitudes, actions)?

_____

_____

3. AFFIRM the Truth.

Read aloud each of the Truths listed on page 132. Which of these Truths do you particularly need to embrace at this time?

_____

Renew your mind (your thinking) by the Word of God. Read the following passages aloud. What do these verses reveal about God's priorities for your life?

Psalm 90:10–12

_____

Matthew 6:25–34

_____

Luke 10:38–42

_____

1 Timothy 5:9–10

_____

Titus 2:4–5 (married women)

_____

1 Corinthians 7:29–35 (unmarried women)

_____

4. ACT on the Truth.

What specific step(s) of action do you need to take to align your life with the Truth?

_____

_____

5. ASK God to help you walk in the Truth.

Father, I confess that I often fill my life with things that are earthly and temporal. I want to spend my life being and doing what is pleasing to You. May the things that matter most to You matter most to me. May Your Word be a light to show me Your agenda for each season of my life. Help me to be sensitive to Your Spirit and to know what is on Your "to do" list for each day of my life. Please show me how to fulfill my distinctive calling and priorities as a woman. Give me the wisdom and courage to eliminate from my schedule any activities that are not Your will for me at this time. Help me to live my life in the light of eternity. And may I be able to say at the end of my life, as Jesus did, "I have brought you glory on the earth by completing the work you gave me to do" (John 17:4). In Jesus' name. Amen.

CHAPTER SIX

LIES WOMEN BELIEVE... ABOUT MARRIAGE

Dear diary,

Things are pretty quiet around the house at the moment—mostly because Adam and I aren't exactly on speaking terms. We had a big argument last night. I should've seen it coming. The day got off to a rough start. He had been up all night helping a cow give birth. Then he had to leave before breakfast to get the rest of the hay stored.

When he finally got home, he was hot and sweaty, exhausted, and not in the greatest mood. I had been cooped up in the house all day with two sick kids, and when he asked why dinner wasn't ready, I suggested that if he wanted dinner maybe he'd better fix it himself. I don't know why I chose that moment to remind him of several chores I wished he would take care of—including clearing out the path in front of the house; it looks like a jungle with all the weeds.

One thing led to another—he had told Abel he could go on a special hunting trip with him next week. I feel he's too young, and besides, I don't think he should take Abel and leave Cain behind. He wouldn't back down, and things got pretty tight. We both said a lot of things we probably shouldn't have said. I went to bed early and pretended I was asleep when he came in.

You'd think after all these years together we ought to have this marriage thing down. Funny thing is, for the most part, I think Adam would say our marriage is doing fine. But sometimes I feel like we're total strangers—even though we've known each other all our lives. He always thinks he's right about everything. When I ask him to try and see things from my point of view, he says nothing will make me happy. I just wish he would be more sensitive to my feelings.

What took place in the Garden of Eden thousands of years ago was not only an attack on God and on two people, it was an attack on marriage. Marriage was designed by God to reflect His glory and His redemptive purposes. In undermining that sacred institution, Satan struck a forceful blow at God's eternal plan.

It is no coincidence that Satan launched his insidious plan by approaching a married woman. He lied to her about God, about His character and His Word, and about sin and its consequences. She believed and acted on his lie and then turned to her husband and drew him into sin with her. The implications in their marriage were profound.

Shame replaced freedom. Pretense and hiding replaced transparency and fellowship. The oneness Eve and her husband had experienced in their original state now turned to enmity and animosity —not only toward God, but toward each other.

Instead of providing loving leadership for his wife, the man was now prone to extremes ranging from domineering control to passive detachment. The protection the woman had been granted under her spiritual "head" was removed, and the independent spirit she had exerted toward God now displayed itself toward her husband, leaving her vulnerable to greater deception, sin, and attack. What was intended to be a joyous, fruitful, intimate relationship between a man, a woman, and their God now became a battleground.

And so it has been in every marriage since.

As with every other area of our lives, deception is Satan's greatest instrument in achieving his destructive purposes for marriage. If he can get husbands and wives to believe and act on his lies, he will succeed in putting them in bondage, stealing their joy, and destroying their relationships. His lies are legion, lies such as . . .

21. "I HAVE TO HAVE A HUSBAND TO BE HAPPY."

Like many other lies, this lie is actually a subtle distortion of the Truth.

The Truth is that marriage is good and right, that it is God's plan for most people, and that there can (and ought to) be great joy and blessing in the context of a God-centered marriage. Satan twists the Truth about marriage by suggesting to women that the purpose of marriage is personal happiness and fulfillment, and that they cannot be truly happy without a husband to love them and meet their needs.

Once they have a husband, many women start to believe a variation of this lie: "My husband is supposed to make me happy." Only after years of heartache did "Myrna" recognize the folly of this way of thinking:

⚘

After ten years together, my husband and I split up. I had believed that it was his responsibility to make me happy. It never was, and it never worked. Not only was I in bondage, but he was also.

⚘

The Truth is that the ultimate purpose of marriage is not to make us happy, but to glorify God. Women who get married for the purpose

137

of finding happiness are setting themselves up for almost certain disappointment; they seldom find what they are looking for.

Women who believe they have to have a husband in order to be happy often settle for less than the best that God intended to give them. "Joan" shared with me how believing this lie placed her in bondage and led to painful consequences she had not anticipated:

During my college years, having a boyfriend, a fiancé, and then a husband who was a good man but not committed to Christ was more important to me than waiting upon God and asking Him to bring a strong believer into my life to marry. As a result, we have not been able to grow in Christ together. After twenty-eight years of marriage, we do not do very many things together. My friends are Christians; his friends are beer drinkers. My priority is my children; his priority is his work.

This woman was deceived. She believed she had to have a husband to be happy. She acted on that belief by marrying a man who was not a believer, contrary to the clear teaching of the Word of God. She got what she thought she wanted (a man), but ended up with spiritual leanness in her soul (Psalm 106:15).

Only by recognizing and embracing the Truth can true freedom be found—with or without a husband. Each of the following testimonies illustrates how believing a lie leads to bondage and how countering the lie with the Truth produces freedom:

I always thought I needed a man in my life to make me happy and build my self-esteem. But even after I got married, I still wasn't happy and still had low self-esteem. Knowing and believing that God created me in His image as well as getting my self-worth

from Him has changed my view of myself and freed me from try-
ing to get my needs met through a man's love and acceptance.

I lost my father when I was fourteen and got married at age six-
teen. I see now that I let my husband become my security and my
reason to live. As our children grew up and we had struggles in our
marriage, I was in bondage to the feeling that "I couldn't live
without my husband." The bondage I was in was as strong as any
metal bar over a window. The bars and the locks in my mind had
a secure hold on me. My heart races just remembering that fearful
state. My husband could not tolerate the suffocation I was causing
and started thinking he needed to get out to breathe.

God used some friends to show me that I needed to turn loose
of "Carl" and take hold of Him. Once I did so, I was free. My
husband grew through all this and never did leave. We praise God
all the time for bringing us through to celebrate thirty-six years of
marriage.

I have struggled with the lie that without marriage I have no value,
that perhaps something is wrong with me. Believing this lie has
robbed me of the joy of serving others (because I have been so ab-
sorbed with my own goals) and deprived me of the contentment
that comes from serving and trusting Him.

It has taken me many years to trust that God is sovereign,
that He has a plan for me, and that I can put my energies into
serving Him, performing good works He has ordained and laying
up riches in heaven.

My focus now (at age forty) is to spend my remaining years
taking advantage of the many opportunities to serve Him and al-
lowing Him to change me into the most Christlike, feminine
woman I can be. This life is so short. He has helped me have an
eternal perspective so the sorrows and disappointments of this
world can be happily endured.

139

The Truth is that happiness is not found in (or out of) marriage; it is not found in any human relationship. True joy can only be found through Christ.

The Truth is that God has promised to give us everything we need, and if He knows a husband would make it possible for us to bring greater glory to Him, then He will provide a husband.

The Truth is that contentment is not found in having everything we think we want but in choosing to be satisfied with what God has already provided.

The Truth is that those who insist on having their own way often end up with unnecessary heartache, while those who wait on the Lord always get His best.

🍎 22. "IT IS MY RESPONSIBILITY TO CHANGE MY MATE."

Most of us as women are born "fixers." If something is wrong, we've got to fix it. If someone is wrong, we've got to fix him or her. The instinct seems almost irresistible, especially with those who live under our own roof. But the thinking that it is our responsibility to change others invariably leads to frustration and conflict.

In the context of marriage, this lie takes the focus off a wife's own needs and her own walk with the Lord—which she can do something about. Further, it places her focus on someone else's failures and needs—which she may be able to do very little, if anything, about. The fact is, she cannot change her husband's (or her children's) heart. However, she can cooperate with the Holy Spirit in changing her own heart.

When a wife is preoccupied with trying to correct her husband's faults and flaws, she is taking responsibility God never intended her to have, and she will likely end up frustrated and resentful toward her husband and perhaps even toward God. She may also limit God from doing what He wants to do in changing her husband. I sometimes wonder how many husbands God would change if their wives were willing to let God take over the process.

Many Christian wives do not realize that they have two power-ful "weapons" available to them that are far more effective than nag-ging, whining, or preaching. The first weapon is a godly life, which God often uses in a man's life to create conviction and spiritual hunger (see 1 Peter 3:1–4).

The second weapon is prayer. When a wife consistently points out the things she wishes her husband would change, she is likely to make him defensive and resistant. But when she takes her concerns to the Lord, she is appealing to a higher power to act in her husband's life—and it's a lot harder for a man to resist God than to resist a nagging wife!

I love the example of Mary, the mother of Jesus, in this regard. An angel appeared and told her she was going to be the mother of the Messiah—an incredible experience. But you had to be there! When she told Joseph what had happened, initially he apparently did not believe her explanation. He hadn't seen any angel. Reason led him to conclude that she had been unfaithful to him.

There is no indication that Mary pressured Joseph to believe what she knew God had told her. Rather, she waited on God and gave Him the opportunity to communicate directly to her husband—which is exactly what happened. Once the angel appeared to Joseph, he was quick to respond and believe. Mary was a woman who knew how to keep things in her heart and ponder them (see Luke 2:19). She could afford to wait and be quiet because she knew the power of God and trusted Him to fulfill His plans for her life and her family.

A woman I had not seen for nearly seventeen years came up to me at a wedding recently and said, "You saved my marriage!" I asked her to refresh my memory. She reminded me that all those years ago she had shared with me her concern in relation to her husband's spir-itual condition. She said, "You told me, 'It's not your responsibility to change your husband; that's God's responsibility. Tell your hus-band what is on your heart and then back off and let God do the rest.'" She continued, "For all these years, I have practiced that ad-vice and have shared it with many other wives."

She went on to tell me what it had meant for her to wait on the

Lord to change her husband. For *sixteen long years,* she had prayed and waited, without seeing any evidence that God was hearing or answering her prayers. Though her husband professed to be a Christian, based on the lack of any spiritual hunger or fruit in his life she questioned whether or not he had a relationship with the Lord at all.

Then, "unexplainably," after all those years, the Spirit turned on the light and brought about a dramatic change in her husband. It was as though he had come out of a coma. All of a sudden, he couldn't get enough of the Word; he started keeping a notepad with him to record the things God was saying to him through the Word. She said, "Before this change, I could hardly get him out of bed for breakfast. Now, he's going to a men's prayer meeting at six-thirty every morning!" Recently, he has even talked about the possibility of selling his business so they can spend more time in some form of ministry. There is no human explanation for what happened to change this husband—except God and a faithful wife who learned how to really pray for her husband.

23. "MY HUSBAND IS SUPPOSED TO SERVE ME."

In the past couple of decades, there has been a significant movement challenging men to become men of God, to love their wives and children, and to express that love through sacrifice and service. What an encouragement it has been to see God stirring men and turning their hearts toward Him and toward their homes. However, in the midst of this emphasis, we women need to be careful that we do not lose sight of the primary roles God has given us to fulfill. In today's evangelical world, it is "politically correct" to challenge men to go home and serve their wives. However, it is not "P.C." to talk to women about their responsibility to serve their husbands.

The Truth is that God did not make the man to be a "helper" to the woman. He made the woman to be a "helper" to the man. Of course, this does not mean that men are not to serve their wives and children. If men are to love their wives as Christ loved the church, there must be the willingness to lay down their lives and become servants, even as Christ did for His bride.

But if we as women focus on what we "deserve," on our "rights," or on what men "ought" to do for us, we will become vulnerable to hurt and resentment when our expectations are not fulfilled. Blessing and joy are the fruit of seeking to be a giver rather than a taker and of looking for ways to bless, serve, and minister to the needs of our families.

In large measure, our thinking as women has been shaped by the modern-day feminist movement, which has made a concerted effort to demean the value of women serving in practical ways in their homes. In her excellent book, *The Feminist Gospel,* Mary Kassian refers to a 1974 study done by sociologist Ann Oakley, analyzing the topic of housework:

> Oakley . . . endeavored to statistically reveal the appalling nature of women's working conditions—arduous work, for long hours, in isolation, with little or no pay, no compensation, no pension, no relief, no time off, no paid holidays, and no basis for negotiation for improved conditions. . . . Oakley sought to   prove that the role of housewife— in housework and child care—was exploitative and oppressive. . . . According to Oakley, a feminist revolt would not be accomplished until women realized they were oppressed.[1]

My mother was one such "oppressed" woman. When I was asked to contribute a chapter for a book on mothers and daughters, this is how I described the example of my mother's life:

> Though an extraordinarily gifted woman in her own right, my mother gladly laid down a promising career as a vocalist in order to take on the position of a "helper suitable" to her husband.
>
> . . . In the climate of the 60s, where women were encouraged to pursue independence, careers, personal recognition, and self-satisfaction, my mother modeled a different role—one in which a woman adapts to the heart and calling of her husband. Rather than expecting her

husband's life to revolve around her needs and interests, her lifestyle revolved around her husband's. . . .

It is important to understand that this "helper" role was not something my dad demanded of my mother; neither was it a position that she accepted grudgingly or reluctantly. She truly adored this man and found delight in walking through life as his partner and encourager.

Mother gladly managed the domestic affairs of a very active household, so as to free him up to better fulfill God's calling for his life. Many women today would consider this lifestyle oppressive. But my mother was far from downtrodden. To the contrary, my father cherished and highly esteemed the partner God placed by his side and delighted to see her maximize her God-given potential and abilities.[2]

The Truth is that we are never more like Jesus than when we are serving Him or others. There is no higher calling than to be a servant.

One of the things that strikes me most about the "virtuous woman" of Proverbs 31 is the fact that she is so utterly selfless. She is not seeking "self-fulfillment"; she isn't interested in advancing "her career," having her own bank account, or being known for her personal accomplishments. To the contrary, she seems virtually unconcerned about her own interests and needs, choosing instead to focus on how she can meet the practical needs of her husband and children, as well as others in her community. On first reading of this passage, one might be tempted to agree with Ann Oakley's conclusion that homemakers are an oppressed breed. But take a fresh look at this woman:

- She is well-dressed (v. 22).
- She and her family have food to eat and enough to share with others (vv. 15, 20).
- She lives a well-ordered life; she is emotionally stable and free from fear about the future (vv. 21, 25).

- Her husband is crazy about her—he is faithful to her, he feels she is "one in a million" and tells her so, and he brags about her to his friends (vv. 11, 28–29, 31).
- Her children honor and praise her (v. 28).

Doesn't sound like an oppressed woman to me! In fact, what woman wouldn't be overjoyed to have the same rewards? But how did she get all those "benefits"? Not by insisting that her husband roll up his sleeves and help out with the household chores (although there's certainly nothing wrong with men doing so), but by choosing the pathway of servanthood—by making it her number one priority (after her relationship with God) to meet the needs of her family.

"Vicki" describes how God set her free from the deception that she was to expect her husband to serve her:

Several years ago, I was set free from a big lie. I always expected my husband to serve me by helping me with household chores and children. I resented it if he did not do so or if he didn't do it well enough; I resented picking up after him or doing things to help or serve him. I had always known that Eve was created as Adam's helpmate, but one day the Holy Spirit personalized this for me and showed me that I had not embraced the role of being a "helper" to my husband.

Now I pick up my husband's socks or newspapers and remind myself that I am "helping" him. I am grateful for all the help he does give me (which really is a lot), and I look for ways to help him accomplish his agenda (free him from jobs around the house, keep kids out of his way, etc.), instead of expecting him to help me accomplish my agenda. It has really helped our marriage.

24. "IF I SUBMIT TO MY HUSBAND, I'LL BE MISERABLE."

A few years ago, a major Protestant denomination ignited a firestorm in the evangelical world when it adopted a statement of biblical beliefs regarding marriage and family that included this sentence:

> A wife is to submit herself graciously to the servant leadership of her husband even as the church willingly submits to the headship of Christ.[3]

The struggle with submission is not unique to women of our day. In fact, that was the essence of the issue Eve faced back in the Garden of Eden. At the heart of the Serpent's approach to Eve was this challenge: Does God have the right to rule your life? Satan said, in effect, "You can run your own life; you don't have to submit to anyone else's authority."

He convinced Eve that if she submitted to God's direction, she would be miserable and would miss out on something in life. From that day to this, Satan has done a masterful job of convincing women that submission is a narrow, negative, and confining concept. He has taken a beautiful, holy, and powerful Truth and made it look ugly, frightening, and undesirable.

Satan knows that if we could see the Truth about biblical submission—one of the most liberating principles in all of God's Word—we would joyfully embrace it. He cannot afford to let us choose the pathway of submission, for when we do, he is stripped of his authority and rendered powerless in our lives and in the lives of those we love.

At the core of fallen human nature (and I believe at the heart of feminist ideology) is a problem with authority. We simply don't want anyone telling us what to do. We want to run our own lives and make our own decisions. Toddlers don't want to be told not to touch breakable items. Teenagers don't want to be told what time to be in at night. We adults don't want anyone telling us we can't drive more than 35 mph on back roads, or that we have to wear a seat belt.

When it comes to submission, the concept of a wife's submitting to her husband's authority is particularly objectionable to many women, including, increasingly, those in our evangelical churches. In part, I believe this is because of a lack of biblical teaching and understanding of the meaning and value of submission. Here again, the variations on Satan's lies are endless.

LIES ABOUT SUBMISSION

1. *"The wife is inferior to her husband."* The Scripture teaches that both the man and the woman are created in the image of God, both have equal value before God, and both are privileged to be subjects of His redeeming grace, through repentance and faith (Genesis 1:27; Galatians 3:28; 1 Peter 3:7). The responsibility of a wife to submit to her husband's authority does not make her any less valuable or significant than her husband.

2. *"As head of his wife, the husband is permitted to be harsh or dictatorial with his wife."* Husbands are commanded to love their wives as they love themselves, in the same selfless, sacrificing, serving way that the Lord Jesus loved His church and laid down His life for it (Ephesians 5:25–29).

3. *"The wife is not to provide input or express her opinions to her husband."* God created the woman to be a "helper suitable" to her husband. That means he needs her help. He needs the input and insight she is able to bring to various situations. It also means that once a wife has graciously and humbly expressed her heart on a matter, if her husband chooses to act contrary to her counsel, she must be willing to back off and trust God with the consequences of her husband's decision.

4. *"The husband is always right."* The apostle Peter specifically addresses women whose husbands "do not believe the word." The husband may be unsaved, or he may be disobedient to God in some area(s) of his life. According to 1 Peter 3:1, the number one means of influencing such a husband is not through tearful pleading, irresistible logic, or persistent reminders; rather, it is through the power of submission:

Wives, in the same way be submissive to your husbands so that, if any of them do not believe the word, they may be won over without words by the behavior of their wives, when they see the purity and reverence of your lives.

1 Peter 3:1–2

THE LIBERATING TRUTH ABOUT SUBMISSION

My perspective on submission has grown as I have come to understand something of God's purpose for authority. God intended that authority should be a means of providing spiritual covering and protection.

When you tell your two-year-old child he may not walk across the busy street outside your house by himself, you are not being tyrannical or cruel; you know there are "cruel" cars on that busy street, and you are acting in your child's best interests. You are using your authority to protect your child (though he may be oblivious to his need for protection).

When we place ourselves under the spiritual covering of the authorities God has placed in our lives, God protects us. On the other hand, when we insist on having it our way and stepping out from under that covering and protection, we open ourselves up to the influence and attack of the Enemy.

I believe the failure of many Christian wives to place themselves under their husbands' authority accounts for the extent to which so many women are vulnerable to Satan's attack on their minds, wills, and emotions. When we come out from under authority—whether in big matters or in seemingly insignificant areas—we become "fair game" for the Enemy.

This is not to suggest that if a wife stays under authority, she will automatically be protected from all suffering or abuse; nor does it mean that abuse is necessarily the result of a woman being out from under rightful authority. According to the Scripture, it is possible for a righteous, submissive person to suffer persecution, which may come in the form of abuse. The book of 1 Peter gives practical insight into God's purposes in suffering and how to respond when we are called to suffer for righteousness' sake.

There are extreme situations where an obedient wife may need to remove herself and/or her children from proximity to her husband, if to remain in that setting would be to place themselves in physical danger. However, even in such a case, a woman can—and must—maintain an attitude of reverence for her husband's position; her goal is not to belittle or resist him as her husband but, ultimately, to see God restore him to obedience. If she provokes or worsens the situation through her attitudes, words, or behavior, she will interfere with what God wants to do in her husband's life and will not be free to claim God's protection and intervention on her behalf.

If you or someone you know is in such a severe situation, ask God to direct you to a source of godly counsel, ideally, one of the elders or spiritual leaders of your church. (There are other factors and means of assistance that may need to be considered in specific situations. The For Further Help section at the back of the book provides additional suggestions for women who are dealing with these types of issues.)

I have discovered that the fundamental issue in relation to submission really comes down to my willingness to trust *God* and to place myself under *His* authority. When I am willing to obey Him, I find it is not nearly so difficult or threatening to submit to the human authorities He has placed in my life.

Proverbs 21:1 assures us that "the king's heart is in the hand of the LORD; he directs it like a watercourse wherever he pleases." Our willingness to place ourselves under God-ordained authority is the greatest evidence of how big we believe God really is.

The Truth is that a higher authority controls every human authority. Ultimately, no human being controls our lives; submission places us in a position of being covered and protected by our wise, loving, all-powerful heavenly Father who controls the "heart of the king."

The question is, do we really believe God is bigger than any human authority? Do we believe He is big enough to change that authority's heart if necessary? Do we believe He is big enough to protect us if we take our rightful place under authority? Do we believe He knows what is best for us, and are we willing to trust Him to fulfill His perfect, eternal purposes for our lives?

The Truth, as we have seen in 1 Peter 3:1–2, is that a wife's submission to her husband makes room for God to work in his heart and bring him to obedience. Peter goes on to say that a submissive heart attitude produces in a woman the most radiant and lasting kind of beauty:

> Your beauty . . . should be that of your inner self, the
> unfading beauty of a gentle and quiet spirit,
> which is of great worth in God's sight.
> For *this is the way the holy women of the past who put
> their hope in God used to make themselves beautiful.
> They were submissive to their own husbands,* like Sarah,
> who obeyed Abraham and called him her master.
> You are her daughters if you do what is right
> and do not give way to fear.
>
> 1 Peter 3:3–6 (italics added)

A wife's submission to her husband, regardless of his spiritual condition, actually releases her from fear because she has entrusted herself to God, who has ultimate control of her husband and her situation.

In her rich book *The True Woman,* Susan Hunt sums up the heart behind submission:

> I cannot give logical arguments for submission. It defies logic that Jesus would release all the glories of heaven so He could give us the glory of heaven. Submission is not about logic; it is about love.
>
> Jesus loved us so much that He voluntarily submitted to death on a cross. His command is that wives are to submit to their husbands. It

is a gift that we voluntarily give to the man we have vowed to love in obedience to the Savior we love. . . .

God said that man needs a helper. The true woman celebrates this calling and becomes affirming rather than adversarial, compassionate rather than controlling, a partner rather than a protagonist. She becomes substantively rather than superficially submissive.

The true woman is not afraid to place herself in a position of submission. She does not have to grasp; she does not have to control. Her fear dissolves in the light of God's covenant promise to be her God and to live within her. Submission is simply a demonstration of her confidence in the sovereign power of the Lord God. Submission is a reflection of her redemption.[4]

25. "IF MY HUSBAND IS PASSIVE, I'VE GOT TO TAKE THE INITIATIVE, OR NOTHING WILL GET DONE."

When we asked women which of the lies in this book they had believed, this lie ranked number three. I know of few subjects that are a greater source of frustration to women than "passive men." Once again, this is not a new struggle. As is true of many issues, it all goes back to the Garden of Eden:

> When the woman saw that the fruit of the tree was good
> for food . . . , she took some and ate it. She also gave some
> to her husband, *who was with her,* and he ate it.

Genesis 3:6 (italics added)

This passage evokes a troubling picture in my mind. The couple is together in the Garden. The Serpent approaches them, ignores the man, and strikes up a conversation with the woman, fully aware that God has placed her under the authority of her husband and that both of them are under God's authority. (Notice Satan's strategy to subvert God's authority structure by going directly to the woman.) Satan starts the exchange by asking her a question: "Did God really say, 'You must not eat from any tree in the garden'?" (Genesis 3:1).

At this point, notice what the woman does *not* do. She does not acknowledge her husband, who is standing by her side. She does not say to the Serpent, "I'd like for you to meet my husband." She does not turn to her husband and ask, "Honey, how do *you* think we should respond?" or "Adam, why don't you tell him what God said to you." She carries on the entire conversation with the Serpent as if her husband were not there.

Further, when it comes time to make a choice, she takes matters into her own hands. She does not consult with her husband on the matter; she does not ask his input or direction; she simply acts: "She took some and ate it" (v. 6).

And what is Adam doing this whole time? He is doing what a lot of women tell me their husbands do much of the time: *Nothing*. He doesn't interfere; he doesn't get involved—except to eat some fruit himself when his wife gives it to him. All of a sudden, we have the first role reversal.

God created the man first and gave him the responsibility to *lead and feed* those under his care. The woman, created from the man, was made to be a receiver, to respond to the initiative of her husband. Even the physiological differences between men and women express this fundamental difference.

But who is leading and feeding in this account? Not the man, but the woman. And who is responding? Not the woman, but the man. Something is wrong with this picture. And ever since, the same thing has been wrong with the sons and daughters of this first couple. That role reversal became the pattern for the way fallen men and women relate to each other.

Ever since that fateful day in Eden, the natural drive of the woman has been to control her husband, to rule over him, and to act independently of him.[5] Our natural tendency is to take the reins, to take the initiative ourselves; ironically, however, because of the way God created us, we also long to be responders; we long for our men to take action.

As was true with Adam and Eve in the Garden, our instinct is to blame the other party for this problem. As women, we are quick to fault men for being passive and to insist that if they weren't so inactive—if they would *just do something*—we would not take matters into our own hands.

Over the years, women have insisted to me that their husbands' passivity has "forced" them to take over:

- "My husband won't work. If I didn't go out and get a job, we would starve to death!"
- "If I let my husband take the lead in financial matters, he would drive us into bankruptcy."
- "He just won't get involved in the children's lives. If I didn't discipline them and make them do right, they would be out of control."

Being something of an activist myself, I know what it is to be frustrated by apparent passivity on the part of some men. I have sat in numerous meetings over the years—with godly men present—biting my tongue to keep from jumping in and taking over when I did not feel the men were being decisive enough.

But as I have watched men and women interact and have evaluated the effect of my own reactions in these sorts of settings, I can't help but wonder to what extent we women have demotivated and emasculated the men around us by our quickness to take the reins rather than waiting on the Lord to move men to action. We can so easily strip men of the motivation to rise to the challenge and provide the necessary leadership. To make matters worse, when they do take action, the women they look to for encouragement and affirmation correct them or tell them how they could have done it better.

I remember hearing one husband talk about how, years earlier, when he and his wife were first married, he led her in a time of prayer.

When they were finished, she began to criticize the way he had prayed. Not surprisingly, this husband said, years later, "I decided that was the last time I would pray with her." He couldn't handle the rejection of his manhood. Not until years later, when God did a fresh work of grace in his heart, did he get the courage to risk stepping out again to lead his wife.

The fact is, in most cases, if the woman is going to take charge, the man is going to stand by and let her. As Elizabeth Rice Handford points out,

> Most men hate "scenes." They despise confusion and disorder. They will go to almost any length to have peace in their homes. They will let a woman have her way rather than argue and quarrel. But the price a man has to pay is the price of his manhood. Before you complain that your husband won't take the leadership of your home, search your heart carefully. Do you really rely on his judgment? Are you willing to commit yourself to his decisions? If not, don't complain that he will not lead. For the sake of peace, he may not fight for his authority.[6]

We simply can't have our cake and eat it, too. We can't insist on running the show and then expect men to be proactive, take initiative, and be "spiritual leaders."

At times, I have asked women who are frustrated by the inactivity of their husbands, "What would happen if you didn't jump in to handle the situation?" You think you have to go to work because he won't get a job? If he gets hungry, he will probably work! You feel you have to take charge of the finances because he is irresponsible with money? He may go bankrupt. But that may be exactly what it takes for God to get his attention and change his character. You must be willing to let him fail—believing that ultimately, your security is not in your husband but in a sovereign God who is not going to fail you.

Sarah is lifted up in the Bible as an example of a woman who reverenced and obeyed her husband. However, on at least one occasion, when God did not act as quickly as she felt He should, she fell into the trap of trying to handle matters on her own. Ten years earlier, God had promised her husband, Abraham, that he would have many descendants and that they would become a great nation. Now she was seventy-six years old and still childless. Impatient with waiting, she decided someone had to do something, so she put pressure on her husband to take action:

> She had an Egyptian maidservant named Hagar;
> so she said to Abram, "The LORD has kept me
> from having children. Go, sleep with my maidservant;
> perhaps I can build a family through her."
> Abram agreed to what Sarai said.
>
> *Genesis 16:1–2*

Sarah resorted to a common practice of the day, by which a barren woman could get a child through one of her own servants. At first, Sarah's plan seemed to work splendidly—Hagar quickly conceived a child. But it didn't take long for the situation to turn sour; the relationship between the childless wife and the expectant servant became unbearable, leading Sarah to go back to Abraham and say, "*You* are responsible for the wrong I am suffering" (Genesis 16:5, italics added).

Thirteen years later, when Sarah was ninety years old, God supernaturally intervened to give Abraham and his wife a child of their own. Isaac was to bring great blessing to the elderly couple and to every future generation yet to be born. But Ishmael, the son born of Abraham and Hagar's union, became a lifelong source of conflict and grief. How many times must Sarah have looked back in regret and said to herself, "Why couldn't I have waited on the Lord? Why did I have to take control of the situation?"

We can take matters into our own hands and may even be able to achieve immediate results. But we usually end up with a bitter taste in our mouths, even resenting and blaming those we feel pushed us into taking action.

What can free us from the drive to control the men in our lives? We must learn to *wait on the Lord;* in His time, and in His way, He will act on behalf of those who wait for Him.

> *Wait on the Lord:* be of good courage, and he shall strengthen thine heart: wait, I say, on the LORD.
>
> Psalm 27:14 *(KJV, italics added)*

26. "SOMETIMES DIVORCE IS A BETTER OPTION THAN STAYING IN A BAD MARRIAGE."

The Enemy often leads us to believe that there is no "right" way to deal with a seemingly hopeless situation. This deception has fostered a culture of shattered marriages.

The fact is, marriage is hard, and good marriages are even harder. Every married couple is "incompatible"—if for no other reason than that men and women are vastly different, not to speak of the fact that every marriage involves two people who are naturally selfish. Any two people living under the same roof are going to be insensitive at times; they are going to hurt each other; there is going to be misunderstanding; they are going to fail to meet each other's needs. The only place where people get married and "live happily ever after" is in fairy tales. Never, since Genesis 3, has there been such a thing as an easy or pain-free marriage.

No sooner does a couple say, "I do," than the Serpent rears his ugly head and sets out to destroy that marriage. He knows every divorce is an attack on the character of God and on the earthly picture of divine redemption. Before the wedding reception is over, Satan is looking for opportunities to plant seeds of deception in the hearts of the newlyweds.

The deception doesn't usually start with full-blown lies—most of those would be quickly rejected. It starts with partial truths, mixed with partial deception; it starts subtly, with thoughts that *appear* to be true and emotions that *feel* true.

So your brand-new husband forgets the two-year anniversary of the day you first met. Or he . . .

- shows up an hour late for a date and forgets to call;
- agrees for the two of you to work in the preschool department at church, without talking with you first;
- tells his parents you'll be there for Christmas, when you were hoping to spend Christmas with your parents;
- or any one of a thousand other "offenses".

To nurse the offense, rather than choosing to forgive and release it, is to become vulnerable to deception that grows bigger and stronger with the passing of time:

- He's always inconsiderate.
- He doesn't care that he hurt me.
- He's impossible to live with.
- He'll never be any different.
- _____ [some other man at work or at church] is so much more thoughtful and considerate. He doesn't treat *his* wife that way.
- There's no way this marriage can work.
- I'd be happier if I were married to _____ [the "other" man].
- If my husband doesn't love and respect me, I have the right to leave him.
- Sometimes two people just can't make a marriage work— apparently, we weren't meant for each other.

- I'm better off getting a divorce than staying in a miserable marriage.
- I don't have any alternative. There's just no way I can stay married to him.

The wife in this scenario has convinced herself that her husband is totally (or mostly) at fault. She is blind to the needs or faults in her own life—or at least she isn't as bothered by her faults as she is by his. She sees his faults through a microscope and her own through a telescope. She doesn't see herself as a sinner, equally in need of God's grace.

Further, her life revolves around herself—her happiness and her hurts. She is more interested in getting her problems solved and her needs met than in the process of restoration and sanctification—in her life, as well as her husband's life. She does not have a vision for how God could use her as an instrument of grace in her husband's life—or she is unwilling to pay the price to be that instrument.

Most importantly, she has left God out of the picture. She does not see His holy purposes for her marriage. Nor does she see how her husband's flaws and the difficulties in her marriage could contribute toward those purposes. She is not exercising faith in the supernatural power of God to transform her and her husband and this marriage into something of great beauty and worth. In wanting to bail out of the marriage, she is elevating her personal happiness and well-being above what God has to say about the permanence of marriage vows and the seriousness of breaking those vows.

It is this kind of thinking that led "Annette" to conclude:

I have a right to be happy. My life is at least half over, and I deserve to spend the rest of it in wedded bliss with someone who will love and cherish me—obviously not my husband.

Years of compounded hurt, if not dealt with God's way, can lead a person to rationalize things they thought they would never believe and to justify choices they thought they would never make. The hardness of heart and the hopelessness that result are the telltale evidence that they have fallen into the Deceiver's trap and have been ensnared by his deception.

The only way to break the cycle and be set free is to reject the lies that have taken over the mind and emotions and to counter those lies with the Truth, as God has revealed it in His Word. The Truth is . . .

- There is no marriage God cannot heal. There is no person God cannot change.
- The primary purpose of marriage is not to be happy, but to glorify God and reflect His redeeming, covenant love.
- God uses the rough edges of each partner in a marriage to conform the other to the image of Christ. Your mate's weaknesses can become a tool in God's hand to make you into the woman He created you to be.
- True love—God's love—is unconditional and never fails. We cannot love another human being perfectly on our own. But God can love anyone through us, if we are willing to let Him. Love is not a feeling; it is a commitment to act in the best interests of another. By God's grace, we can choose to love anyone, even if we do not have warm feelings toward that person.
- Marriage is a covenant. God is a covenant-keeping God. He kept His promises to the nation of Israel, even when they were spiritually adulterous and pursued other lovers (see Jeremiah 11:10; Ezekiel 20:16; Hosea 2:13). The Lord Jesus keeps His promises to His bride—the church—even when we are unfaithful to Him. Because He is faithful to keep His promises, it is never right for us to break the marriage covenant that was intended to be a picture of the redemptive relationship between God and His people.

- God has commanded us to forgive without limit.
- Your faithfulness and willingness to extend sacrificial love to your mate may be the means of his spiritual healing, even as Christ's suffering was the means by which we were healed (1 Peter 2:24–25; 1 Corinthians 7:12–14).
- You don't solve your problems by putting another pair of shoes under the bed. (Statistically, second marriages have a higher divorce rate than first marriages.)
- God's grace is sufficient to enable you to be faithful to your mate and to love and forgive without limit.
- God will never forsake you. Regardless of what you must endure, He will be there to carry you through.
- The rewards of faithfulness in this life may not be fully experienced until eternity. But faithfulness *will be rewarded* and it will be worth the wait!

Years ago, a woman handed me a piece of paper after hearing me speak at a conference. The handwriting at the top read:

Forgiveness is the only way to receive God's best!

There followed a series of single sentences that outlined the touching story of this woman's pilgrimage from deception to truth—from bondage to freedom.

- Many years ago, my husband wronged me.
- I filed for divorce.
- I received a note from a friend whose wife had died. His note said simply, "Humble yourself."
- I did so—unhappily, unwillingly.
- The more I humbled myself and sought to love my husband, the more he became a wonderful man of God.
- I became proud to be his wife. I actually enjoyed it! (A lot.)

- One Christmas Eve, we held each other in amazement. God had restored *all* aspects of our marriage beyond what we ever dreamed.
- December 26—we prayed together and embraced. I kissed him good-bye. One hour later, he was dead.
- God gave me a gift of *no regret*. As hard as it is to live without him, it is easy, because there is no regret.
- I would say to a married woman: Don't waste precious time receiving God's best for your life. Humble yourself. Give your husband room and time to be God's man. It takes time and sacrifice, but the blessing is amazing!

The Enemy has made a mess and a mockery out of marriage. His lies have resulted in countless fractured lives and homes. Only the Truth has power to redeem, restore, and renew.

THE LIE	THE TRUTH
21. I HAVE TO HAVE A HUSBAND TO BE HAPPY.	• Happiness is not found in (or out of) marriage. • There is no person who can meet my deepest needs. No one and nothing can make me truly happy, apart from God. • God has promised to provide everything I need. If He will receive more glory by my being married, then He will provide a husband for me. • Those who wait on the Lord always get His best. Those who insist on getting what they want often end up with heartache.
22. IT IS MY RESPONSIBILITY TO CHANGE MY MATE.	• A godly life and prayer are a wife's two greatest means of influencing her husband's life. • It is far more effective for a woman to appeal to the Lord to change her husband than to try to exert pressure on him directly.
23. MY HUSBAND IS SUPPOSED TO SERVE ME.	• If I expect to be served, I will often be disappointed. If I seek to serve others, without expecting anything in return, I will never be disappointed. • God made the woman to be a helper to the man. • We are never more like Jesus than when we are serving others.
24. IF I SUBMIT TO MY HUSBAND, I'LL BE MISERABLE!	• Submission places me under the covering and protection of God, who controls the "heart of the king." • When I step out from under authority, I become vulnerable to the attacks of the Enemy.

THE LIE	THE TRUTH
	• My willingness to place myself under God-ordained authority is the greatest evidence of how big I believe God really is.
	• Reverent submission is a wife's greatest means of influencing a husband who is not walking with God.
	• A wife's response to her husband's authority should demonstrate the way the church is to submit to the authority of the Lord Jesus.
25. IF MY HUSBAND IS PASSIVE, I'VE GOT TO TAKE THE INITIATIVE, OR NOTHING WILL GET DONE.	• God created the man to be an initiator and the woman to be a responder.
	• If a woman takes the reins rather than waiting on God to move her husband, her husband is likely to be less motivated to fulfill his God-given responsibility.
26. SOMETIMES DIVORCE IS A BETTER OPTION THAN STAYING IN A BAD MARRIAGE.	• Marriage is a lifelong covenant that is intended to reflect the covenant-keeping heart of God. As He is faithful to His covenant, so we must be faithful to keep our marriage covenant.
	• There is no marriage God cannot heal. There is no person God cannot change.
	• God uses the rough edges of each partner in a marriage to conform the other to the image of Christ.
	• God's grace is sufficient to enable you to be faithful to your mate and to love and forgive without limit.

1. AGREE with God.

What lies have you believed about marriage?

_____

_____

2. ACCEPT responsibility.

How has believing those lies manifested itself in the way you live (e.g., attitudes, actions)?

_____

_____

3. AFFIRM the Truth.

Read aloud each of the Truths listed on pages 162–63. Which of these Truths do you particularly need to embrace at this time?

_____

Renew your mind (your thinking) by the Word of God. Read the following passages aloud. What do these verses reveal about God's perspective on marriage in general and a wife's role in particular?

Mark 10:6–9

_____

Proverbs 31:10–12

_____

Ephesians 5:22–24, 32–33

_____

1 Peter 3:1–6

_____

4. ACT on the Truth.

What specific step(s) of action do you need to take to align your life with the Truth?

_____

_____

5. ASK God to help you walk in the Truth.

My Father, I thank You for designing the institution of marriage. Thank You for the earthly picture it provides of Your covenant love, Your great plan of redemption, and the relationship the Lord Jesus has with His church. Please show me where I have embraced or even promoted a perspective of marriage that is not completely biblical. I confess that even the best human marriages fall far short of all that You intended, for we are proud, self-centered people. I thank You for Your grace that can enable men to love and lead their wives as Christ loves and leads His bride, and can enable women to reverence and submit to their husbands as the church is to respond to her Bridegroom.

[Married women]: Because You are faithful to Your covenant, I commit myself to be faithful to my husband as long as we both live. Please help me to love him as You command (Titus 2:4), to forgive and forbear his weaknesses, to honor him as my head, and to submit to him in such a way that others will be drawn to submit themselves to Christ. Grant me to be clothed with a pure, gentle, quiet spirit, so that in areas where my husband may not be walking in obedience, he may be won over to You.

[Unmarried women]: Show me how to encourage, protect, and guard the marriages of others. Keep me pure, and may I never violate the sacredness of someone else's marriage covenant. Thank You for Jesus, who is my heavenly Bridegroom. May I be fully devoted to Him, may I seek to cultivate oneness with Him, and may I be content with all that I have in Him.

In Jesus' name. Amen.

CHAPTER SEVEN

LIES WOMEN BELIEVE... ABOUT CHILDREN

Dear diary,

Adam has been talking about having another child. I'm not so sure about the idea. I love our sons more than anything else in the world. But being a mother is hard work!

There has been a lot of tension between the boys recently. Cain never seems to feel that he measures up to his younger brother. It's like he's got something to prove. His attitude has gone from bad to worse. He has been unusually withdrawn and at times becomes sullen and depressed. He just won't communicate. I keep trying to affirm him, but nothing I say seems to help. He used to be so close to God, but now he says he's not sure he even believes in God.

His dad gets pretty frustrated with him at times. They just don't seem to be able to relate. Sometimes I think Adam is too hard on him. I remind him that there was a time when we experienced some of these kinds of struggles ourselves.

As a mother, I feel so helpless to "fix" my children. I'm concerned about how all of this is going to affect Abel. I can't imagine how Adam thinks we could handle another child.

No greater capacity for joy and love or for disappointment and pain can be found than in a mother's heart. Whether her offspring is a star athlete or trips over his own feet, whether he is an intellectual giant or mentally handicapped, whether he grows up to become a corporate CEO or a hardened criminal, she never stops hoping, dreaming, and longing for that child she once cradled in her arms.

It is in this most sensitive of relationships—with their own flesh and blood—that many women find themselves particularly vulnerable to deception. As in every other area, Satan has a vast arsenal of lies that he uses to deceive a woman in relation to her children and her role as a mother.

Satan's intent in promoting these lies is not only to place mothers in bondage, but also to pass his deception down to the next generation, so they will never know the Truth or experience its liberating power.

In this chapter, we want to focus on a number of subtle lies and half-truths that have become widely accepted in our contemporary Christian culture. These faulty ways of thinking have created costly consequences in our Christian homes—consequences that will be even further magnified in future generations if we do not recognize and reject the lies and replace them with the Truth.

🍎 27. "IT'S UP TO US TO DETERMINE THE SIZE OF OUR FAMILY."

This morning a friend in another state told me that she is expecting her fourth child. She and her husband are delighted by the news; however, they are discovering that not everyone shares their enthusiasm. "In fact," she told me, "some of the most critical comments we have heard are from people in our church."

My friend admitted that these negative responses have caused her to wonder at moments, "Am *I* the one who has lost my mind?"

God is the Creator, Author, and Giver of life. Not surprisingly, as the sworn enemy of God, Satan hates life. He has always sought to destroy it. He persuaded Adam and Eve to eat of the forbidden fruit, knowing that if they did, they would die, as God had promised. When Adam and Eve gave birth to two sons, Satan incited the elder of the two to murder his younger brother.

Satan is the thief Jesus spoke of who "comes only to steal and *kill and destroy*" (John 10:10, italics added). His intent and strategy are precisely the opposite of God's plan, for in the same verse Jesus says, "I have come that they may have *life,* and have it to the full."

As a destroyer of life, Satan is definitely not into encouraging childbearing. Every child that is born has the potential to thwart his purposes by receiving God's grace and becoming a subject of the kingdom of God. So anything that hinders or discourages women from fulfilling their God-given calling to be bearers and nurturers of life furthers Satan's efforts.

Abortion, infanticide, and homosexuality are examples of life-destroying practices that have become widely tolerated throughout our culture. Bible-believing Christians are generally quick to refute such blatantly evil practices. However, the evangelical world—including many outspoken "pro-lifers"—has come to accept a number of philosophies and practices that are subtly "antichildren" and "antilife."

One of the fundamental tenets of feminist ideology has always been the right of a woman to determine for herself if and when she will have children and how many children she will have. Shulamith Firestone, a popular feminist thinker and writer in the 1960s and 1970s, spoke for the movement when she insisted: "The heart of woman's oppression is her childbearing and childrearing roles."[1]

The Christian world has been unwittingly influenced by this way of thinking, leading to the legitimization and promotion of such practices as contraception, sterilization, and "family planning." As a result, unwittingly, millions of Christian women and couples have helped to further Satan's attempts to limit human reproduction and thereby destroy life.

As Mary Pride points out in her penetrating book *The Way Home,*

> Family planning is the mother of abortion. A generation had to be indoctrinated in the ideal of planning children around personal convenience before abortion could become popular. We Christians raise an outcry against abortion today, and rightly so. But the reason we have to fight those battles today is because we lost them thirty years ago. Once couples began to look upon children as creatures of their own making, who they could plan into their lives as they chose or not, all reverence for human life was lost. . . .
>
> . . . Abortion is first of all a heart attitude. "Me first." "My career first." "My reputation first." "My convenience first." "My financial plans first." And these exact same choices are what family planning, which the churches have endorsed for three decades, is all about.[2]

The process by which most people—even "believers"—determine the size of their family is often driven by fear, selfishness, and natural, human reason:

- "How will we ever provide for more children? We're barely making ends meet, as it is. What about college tuition?"
- "I can't physically handle more children. I'm exhausted trying to take care of the two I already have."
- "I just don't have the patience to handle a lot of children."
- "If we have more children, we won't have enough time for us as a couple."
- "My friends [or parents] will think we're crazy if we have more kids. They already think we have too many."
- "If we were to let the Lord decide how many children we should have, we'd have two dozen kids!"

The world says, "Children are a burden." God's Word says children are one of the greatest blessings He can give a couple (Psalm 127:3–5). Yet we look up to heaven and say, "God, please don't send any more blessings!"

The world says, "The purpose of marriage is to make you happy. That may or may not include having children." God's Word, on the other hand, teaches that one of the vital purposes of marriage is to produce children who fear and reverence the Lord (Malachi 2:15).

In the apostle Paul's first epistle to Timothy, we are reminded that childbearing is a basic, God-given role for women. Paul exhorts younger widows to "marry, to *have children,* to manage their homes and to give the enemy no opportunity for slander" (1 Timothy 5:14, italics added). In the last verse of chapter 2, he states, "Women will be saved through childbearing—if they continue in faith, love and holiness with propriety."

Of course, this is not to suggest that a woman's eternal salvation is obtained through childbearing. This verse has the same grammatical construction as Paul's admonition to Timothy in chapter 4, verse 16: "Watch your life and doctrine closely. Persevere in them, because if you do, you will save both yourself and your hearers."

Paul is saying that preaching was Timothy's role, and that perseverance in his calling would accompany genuine conversion. Preaching was not a *means* of Timothy's salvation, but a *necessary fruit* of it. Likewise, a woman's willingness to embrace, rather than shun, her God-given role and calling ("childbearing") is a necessary fruit that will accompany genuine salvation—it is proof that she belongs to Him and follows His ways.

(This is not to say that all women are called by God to marry and bear children, but simply that, generally speaking, this is the central role God has established for women.)

Mary of Nazareth is a beautiful example of a woman who demonstrated faith by her willingness to bear a child, even when it was not in her timing. We can only imagine all the objections that might have gone through the heart of this teenager when the angel announced that she was to give birth to a son:

- "I'm too young! I'm not ready to have a child."
- "I won't be able to spend time with Joseph and my friends if I get tied down with a baby."
- "I want to get settled in my new house first."
- "What will everyone say? No one will understand."
- "We can't afford a child yet. Joseph is just getting his business going."
- "The baby will be born in the middle of Caesar's census, and I won't even be home!"

But there is no indication of any such hesitation or reservation on Mary's part. Her response was simply, *"I am the Lord's servant. . . . May it be to me as you have said"* (Luke 1:38, italics added). She said, in effect, "You are my Lord. I am Your servant. My body is Yours; I accept any inconvenience or hardship this will mean for me. All that matters to me is fulfilling the purpose for which You created me. I gladly surrender myself to be used as You will."

How thankful I am for a mother who responded the same way to God's call in her life. An accomplished musician, when Nancy Sossomon married Art DeMoss at the age of nineteen, they planned to wait at least five years before having children so she could continue her vocal career. However, the Lord had other plans. Within the first five years of their marriage, He gave them six children! At the same time, my mother was helping my dad start a business. Throughout those early years of marriage and childbearing, and then with the addition of a seventh child several years later, she welcomed each child God gave her. I have never heard my mother express anything other than gratitude for the blessing of having children and being a mother.

Mary of Nazareth and my mother—these women are a picture of the Lord Jesus, who welcomed children into His life, took time for them, and urged His followers to do the same (Matthew 19:13–15).

28. "CHILDREN NEED TO GET EXPOSED TO THE 'REAL WORLD' SO THAT THEY CAN LEARN TO FUNCTION IN IT."

If Satan can't keep Christian women from bearing children, he will do his best to deceive them as to how their children ought to be brought up. He uses the same tactics with parents that he used with Eve. He convinced her that by eating the forbidden fruit, she would learn something she needed to know: "When you eat of it your eyes will be opened . . . knowing good and evil" (Genesis 3:5). Satan was right—when Eve ate, her eyes *were* opened (v. 7); she did learn something she had not known before—the experience of evil. The result of this knowledge was shame, guilt, and alienation from God and her husband.

God never intended that you and I should know evil by experiencing it for ourselves. His desire is that we should be "wise about what is good, and innocent about what is evil" (Romans 16:19). But Satan says, "You need to taste for yourself." He says to parents, "Your children need to taste for themselves. If you shelter them from the 'real world,' they will never be able to fit in and survive in it."

The Truth is, our task is not to rear children who can "fit in" or merely "survive" in this world. The challenge of every Christian parent is to bring up children who love God with all their hearts, souls, minds, and strength; who have a vibrant, personal relationship with the Lord Jesus; and whose lives will be bright and shining lights, penetrating the darkness around them. Christian parents ought to be seeking to raise up not just "good" children, but children who enthusiastically embrace the Truth, children who love righteousness and hate evil, children who will be used by God to *change* this world.

I can't thank the Lord enough for guiding my parents to cultivate in us a deep love for holiness and a strong aversion to sin, not so much out of fear of what the culture might do to us, as out of reverence and love for the Lord.

Although they could have afforded to enroll us in one of the fine, private secular schools in our area, they chose instead to place us in a less-established Christian school. Some would have argued that we might have received a better-quality education elsewhere, but my parents understood that "the fear of the Lord is the beginning of wisdom" and that the best preparation for life is to be trained in the Truth of God's Word as it relates to every academic discipline.

They took practical steps to protect our young minds and hearts from exposure to the values and influence of this world system. God gave my mother a strong sense of discernment about some things that many parents wouldn't think twice about today. For example, when almost every other little girl was playing with Barbie dolls, we scarcely knew what they were. She wisely understood that for little girls to play with dolls with fully developed figures would not help to cultivate a godly perspective on sexuality.

When I was a young girl, the nation was in the throes of rebellion, rioting, and revolution. Dissidents voiced their opposition to the war in Vietnam by marching in the streets and burning flags. Millions of young people were getting high on drugs, sex, and rock music. The Supreme Court ruled that women had a constitutional right to have an abortion. Khrushchev was threatening to bury the United States. We were not unaware of these developments, but neither were we hearing about them on the evening news. My parents believed that some topics were not suitable for children's minds to ponder, and they felt responsible to shape our views on what was going on in the world.

The result? I was a very sheltered young person. I don't recall ever hearing a single word of profanity before graduating from high school. I knew virtually nothing about the popular cartoon characters, movies, or television programs of the day.

But, by God's grace and thanks to the influence of godly parents, there are some things I did know that few other young people knew. I knew the difference between right and wrong. I had a good overview of the Scripture—in addition to family devotions and sound doctrinal preaching in church, our elementary school curriculum included two journeys through the entire Bible. I had hidden large portions of Scripture in my heart, had a basic understanding of the major doctrines of the Christian faith, and could sing from memory all the stanzas of many theologically rich hymns. I had read the biographies of many true heroes—men and women such as Hudson Taylor, George Mueller, William Carey, and Gladys Aylward.

Even more important than "knowing" all these things, I had a vital, personal relationship with the Lord Jesus—a relationship that would sustain me when I was out on my own and would motivate me to make right choices once I was outside the protective walls of our home. The "faith of our fathers" had become my own.

I'm not boasting about any of these things—I can't take any credit at all—they were gifts from the Lord and from parents who took seriously their responsibility to raise godly daughters and sons.

Children will cultivate an appetite for whatever they are fed in their earliest, formative years. I have known young people from "committed" Christian homes who know more about movie stars and rock groups than they do about the patriarchs or the disciples. They can sing along with all the top hit songs but do not know the great hymns of the faith. I can only assume that they have an appetite for what they have been exposed to.

If we allow our children to listen to music, attend movies, read books and magazines, and hang out with friends that promote profanity, negative attitudes, illicit sex, rebellion, and violence, we should not be surprised when they adopt the world's philosophies.

As I am writing this chapter, there are about eight inches of snow on the ground, and it has been snowing steadily all day. No one would think of taking a young, tender plant and planting it outside on a day like today and have any hope of its surviving. That's what a greenhouse is for—to provide an optimum environment for plants to grow. Then, when their roots have developed and they are strong enough to withstand adversity, they can be transplanted to the outdoors.

When I was seventeen years old, my parents sent me across the United States to begin my junior year of college at a secular university in southern California. Though I lived with a godly family for those last two years of college, all of a sudden, I had more "freedom" than I had ever had in my life. I could have gone anywhere I wanted to go and done anything I wanted to do. But my "want to" had already been shaped—I loved the Lord and wanted to do what I knew would please Him. My decisions were not driven by fear of what my parents would think but, rather, by a strong sense of the presence, holiness, and love of God.

During those years, I was exposed to philosophies and lifestyles that were foreign to me. But I didn't have an appetite for anything that wasn't consistent with the Word of God. I had a heart for the *people* who believed those things and practiced those lifestyles and wanted to see them come to know the Lord. But their ways held no appeal to me.

I had witnessed firsthand in my home the blessings of fervent love for God and glad-hearted surrender to His ways; that upbringing had cultivated in me a heart to please the Lord and to walk in the Truth.

The apostle Paul warns believers of every era and every culture, "Don't let the world around you squeeze you into its own mould" (Romans 12:2 PHILLIPS). Rather, he says, we are to "make a decisive dedication of [our] bodies as a living sacrifice" (Romans 12:1 WILLIAMS) and to be "transformed by the renewing of [our minds]" (Romans 12:2). We are not to be molded by the culture, as so many believers are today but, rather, are to be so filled with the Spirit and the Word of God that our lives will penetrate and convict the culture around us. That is the challenge facing Christian parents—to raise up a generation of young people who are not conformers but transformers.

29. "ALL CHILDREN WILL GO THROUGH A REBELLIOUS STAGE."

The Enemy wants parents to believe there is no hope of their children living holy, surrendered lives through their adolescent and young adult years. Believing this lie can cause parents to dread, rather than anticipate, their children's teenage years. It can cause them to tolerate or excuse rebellious attitudes and behavior. Children who know their parents expect them to rebel will likely fulfill that expectation.

The fact is, we are *all* natural rebels. Our parents were sinners, we were born sinners, and our children and grandchildren are born with the same inherent bent toward rebellion (Psalms 51:5; 58:3; Isaiah 59:2–8).

That's where the Gospel comes in. As soon as that first pair disobeyed God, He put into place a redemptive plan—a means to rescue them and their children from their rebellion. Through the provision of a sacrifice offered up as a substitute, God made His grace available to fallen sinners.

God's intent was that each successive generation should receive His grace, keep His covenant, and then pass it on to their children. Christian parents have been given a sacred mandate to lead their children to submit their lives to Jesus as Lord and to take their children with them into the "ark of salvation." That high and holy calling is accompanied by the divine resources of His Spirit and His promises.

Sarah Edwards, wife of eighteenth-century New England pastor Jonathan Edwards, was a deeply spiritual woman who sought to believe and act on the Truth in every area of her life. Nowhere was this more apparent than in her role as the mother of eleven children. Jonathan Edwards's *Memoirs* reveals that she approached this challenging calling with confidence and with the commitment to teach her children obedience at the earliest possible age.

> She had an excellent way of governing her children. . . . She had need to speak but once; she was cheerfully obeyed; murmuring and answering again were not known among them. In their manners, they were uncommonly respectful to their parents . . . . Quarreling and contention, which too frequently take place among children, were in her family wholly unknown. . . .Her system of discipline was begun at a very early age, and it was her rule to resist the first, as well as every subsequent, exhibition of temper or disobedience in the child, however young, until its will was brought into submission to the will of its parents; wisely reflecting, that until a child will obey his parents, he can never be brought to obey God.[3]

Recently a mother told me that when her firstborn son was still a child, she began teaching him that just because most young people choose to rebel during their teenage years, that didn't mean he had to do the same. She and her husband have instilled in their three children a vision for how they can be different. They have stressed and are modeling to their children the importance and benefits of choosing the pathway of obedience.

When seeds of rebellion surface, wise parents do not shrug and say, "I guess all kids have to go through this." They understand that their children are experiencing physiological and hormonal changes that may produce emotional ups and downs, but they teach their children how to deal with runaway emotions and how to keep them from ruling their lives. As needed, they deal with issues head-on, with love and firmness, seeking to preserve relationships, to maintain open lines of communication, and to keep pointing their children to the Lord. There are consequences for their children's wrong choices, and there is grace when they repent. This mom and dad are not afraid to model humility and to seek forgiveness when they blow it as parents.

Most of all, they pray earnestly for their children; they trust the Spirit of God to capture their hearts; and they let their teens know that they expect them to pass the baton of God's redemptive covenant on to the next generation.

In the midst of an increasingly rebellious generation, we need parents who see themselves as stewards of His covenant, moms and dads who dare to lay hold of His promises for their children and grandchildren, parents who believe the Truth:

From everlasting to everlasting
the LORD'S love is with those who fear him,
and his righteousness with their children's children. . . .
Then our sons in their youth
will be like well-nurtured plants,
and our daughters will be like pillars
carved to adorn a palace. . . .

All your sons will be taught by the LORD,
and great will be your children's peace.

Psalms 103:17; 144:12; Isaiah 54:13

🍎 30. "I KNOW MY CHILD IS A CHRISTIAN BECAUSE HE PRAYED TO RECEIVE CHRIST AT AN EARLY AGE."

Over the years, countless women have shared with me their concern for a son or daughter who is far from God—a grown child (or grandchild) who has no heart for or interest in spiritual matters and is living a godless lifestyle. These women are convinced, nonetheless, that their children are Christians. The following notes from mothers represent a recurring theme I hear with increasing frequency:

I have a daughter who is a stripteaser and a son who is gay. I want them to come back to the Lord. They both have been saved and baptized.

Neither of my sons is living for the Lord. They accepted Christ as children, but lost it all when they went away to college.

I believe Satan blinds many parents to the true spiritual condition of their children in order to keep those children in bondage to the kingdom of darkness. The parents who are most vulnerable to this lie are those who have raised their children in the church, who have "taught them right from wrong," and whose children have made some sort of profession of faith as a child or young person—they may have even had great interest in spiritual matters at one time. These parents frequently assume that because all of the above is true, their son or daughter must be a genuine Christian.

However, the Scripture is clear that a person may know all about God, say all the right things, and even have deeply religious experiences—without ever being converted. Only God knows anyone's heart. But He has given us some objective standards by which we may measure a profession of faith—whether ours or someone else's. The first epistle of John was written to provide assurance of salvation to those who had been genuinely converted—and to warn those who had no real basis for their profession of salvation. John identifies specific characteristics that distinguish between those who have been truly saved and those who profess to be saved but are merely religious:

> We know that we have come to know him if we obey his commands. The man who says, "I know him," but does not do what he commands is a liar, and the truth is not in him. . . .

> This is how we know we are in him: Whoever claims to live in him must walk as Jesus did. . . .

> Anyone who claims to be in the light but hates his brother is still in the darkness. . . .

> If anyone loves the world, the love of the Father is not in him. . . .

> If they had belonged to us, they would have remained with us; but their going showed that none of them belonged to us. . . .

> This is how we know who the children of God are and who the children of the devil are:

Anyone who does not do what
is right is not a child of God; nor is
anyone who does not love his brother.

1 John 2:3–4, 5b–6, 9, 15b, 19b; 3:10

The essence of true salvation is not a matter of profession or performance; rather, it is a transformation: "If anyone is in Christ, he is a new creation; the old has gone, the new has come!" (2 Corinthians 5:17). The man or woman who has been truly converted has a new life, a new heart, a new nature, a new allegiance, and a new master: "For he has rescued us from the dominion of darkness and brought us into the kingdom of the Son he loves" (Colossians 1:13).

Included in the new covenant is the assurance that we will persevere in our faith. God promises: "I will put My fear in their hearts *so that they will not depart from Me*" (Jeremiah 32:40 NKJV, italics added). And the writer to the Hebrews indicates that perseverance to the end is a mark of true faith: "We have come to share in Christ *if we hold firmly till the end* the confidence we had at first" (Hebrews 3:14, italics added).

The apostle Paul warned the Ephesian believers about those who profess to know Christ but whose lives do not bear the marks of genuine conversion:

For of this you can be sure: No immoral, impure or greedy
person—such a man is an idolater—has any inheritance
in the kingdom of Christ and of God. *Let no one deceive
you with empty words,* for because of such things
God's wrath comes on those who are disobedient.

Ephesians 5:5–6, italics added

For parents to assume that their children have been born again when their lives give no such evidence can have several dangerous results. It can lull those children into a false sense of security about their eternal destiny. It can keep parents from praying appropriately and waging spiritual battle on behalf of their children's souls. It gives rise to a form of "cheap grace" that demeans the person and blood of Christ. It fills our church pews with members who think they are OK. They believe this even though they have no relationship with Christ and their lives are blaspheming the Word of God and causing the world to wonder about what Christianity really is.

It is certainly possible for those who have been truly converted to disobey God or to have a period of backsliding. But no true believer can sin willfully and habitually without experiencing the conviction of God's Spirit.

The Truth is, no matter how "house-trained" a son or daughter (or a mom or dad!) may be in spiritual matters, no matter how fervent they may have appeared to be at one time, if they do not have any heart or hunger for God, if they have a consistent pattern of rejecting the Word and ways of God, they need to be challenged to reconsider whether they were ever really converted in the first place.

31. "WE ARE NOT RESPONSIBLE FOR HOW OUR CHILDREN TURN OUT."

Perhaps the most common type of prayer request women have shared with me over the years is for their wayward children and grandchildren. I could fill a book with the pain and longing expressed by mothers like these:

My sixteen-year-old ran away nine months ago and moved in with her boyfriend—the hurt is so deep.

My twenty-eight-year-old daughter has denied her faith in Christ and is involved in a gay relationship.

Pray that God would break my eighteen-year-old son's heart and deliver him from an addiction (from early childhood) to pornography.

I am struggling with disappointment with my teenage sons, who don't care about the things of the Lord—and with my failure to raise godly children.

Those who have never been there can only imagine the enormous heartache these women carry. I have observed that the Enemy uses two opposite lies to put parents in bondage. The first is that they have no control or influence over how their children have turned out—that they are not responsible, that the situation could not be helped. Believing this lie leads parents to throw off personal responsibility and to feel that they are helpless victims.

The second lie parents believe is that they are 100 percent responsible for how their children have turned out—that it is all their fault. They fail to recognize that, regardless of how well or poorly anyone is parented, each individual must assume responsibility for his or her own choices.

When children rebel, it seems that Satan often causes parents to swing from one of these lies to the other. They are either overwhelmed with shame or they escape into irresponsibility. Both lies are actually subtle distortions of the Truth and can leave parents with a sense of despair and hopelessness.

LIKE FATHER, LIKE SON?

The Scripture includes accounts of godly men who had ungodly children, as well as ungodly men whose children had a heart for God.

Very little explanation is given for why this is so. However, we are given some clues that provide insight for parents who want their children to become true followers of Christ.

The story of Abraham's nephew, Lot, illustrates the influence of a parent's example and values. Lot opted for a lifestyle of ease, affluence, and popularity. His worldly values led him to move his family to a city characterized by arrogance, immorality, and perversion. Is it any wonder, then, that his daughters married men who disdained Lot's spiritual "beliefs" and rejected his pleas to escape the coming judgment? Should it surprise us that after fleeing Sodom, his daughters schemed to get their father drunk and then took turns sleeping with him so they would not be childless?

The New Testament tells us that Lot was a "righteous man." Lot did not personally participate in the outright wickedness of Sodom; in fact, he was "tormented in his righteous soul by the lawless deeds he saw and heard" (2 Peter 2:8). But though he was a believer, he did not guard his heart; he had an appetite for the things of this world. Lot tried to live with one foot in the kingdom of God and one foot in the world. By his example, he led his family into a love affair with the world.

The price Lot paid for his temporal values seems high, but the law of sowing and reaping means that the seed sown will invariably yield a multiplied harvest. As more than one person has pointed out: "What parents tolerate in moderation, their children will excuse in excess."

The account of Eli's family demonstrates the necessity of parents' establishing godly standards for their children's behavior and then exercising the necessary discipline to enforce those parameters. Israel's priest during the dark period of the judges, Eli was a devoted servant of the Lord. Though his two sons, Hophni and Phinehas, grew up in an extremely religious home and setting, the Bible says they were "wicked men" who "had no regard for the LORD" (1 Samuel 2:12).

As sons of a priest, they had little choice but to pursue a career in the priesthood. But they corrupted their sacred calling, they plundered the people by extorting offerings that belonged to the Lord, and they went so far as to engage in sexual relations with the women who served at the tabernacle (1 Samuel 2:13–17, 22). How did a dedicated man of God end up with two such sons? Undoubtedly, they were influenced by the decadent culture around them, but the Scripture tells us some things about their father that apparently contributed to the outcome.

We know that at the time of his death, Eli was overweight (1 Samuel 4:18). Could there be a connection between his lack of physical discipline and his sons' sin of filling their own bellies with meat they had extorted from those who came to offer sacrifices?

The Scripture tells us that on at least one occasion, Eli heard what his sons were doing and confronted them about their wicked behavior (1 Samuel 2:22–25). However, by that time, he was "very old." One can only wonder why he waited so long and whether he had overlooked their behavior prior to that time. At any rate, "his sons . . . did not listen to their father's rebuke" (v. 25). On two subsequent occasions, God sent a messenger to confront Eli about his responsibility in the matter. Though his sons' sin was more blatant and more widely known, the fact is, they were a magnified reflection of their father·

> Why do you scorn my sacrifice and offering . . . ?
> Why do you honor your sons more than me
> by fattening yourselves on the choice parts
> of every offering made by my people Israel? . . .
>
> I told him that I would judge his family forever because
> of the sin he knew about; his sons made themselves
> contemptible, and he failed to restrain them.
>
> *1 Samuel 2:29; 3:13*

Eli paid a heavy toll for his indulgent ways.

These examples do not prove that there is a direct cause-and-effect relationship between parents' spirituality and the spiritual outcome in every child. However, they do illustrate that parents have enormous influence and are responsible to mold the hearts and lives of their children. As easy as it is to shift blame to peers, teachers, entertainment, church youth groups, or secular culture, the fact is, we are accountable for the spiritual condition of the flock God has given us to shepherd.

I want to share my heart with you: I believe many Christian parents are simply blind to the impact of their own example in their children's lives, as well as the decisions they are making (or not making) in relation to their children. I confess to being both amazed and deeply disturbed when I hear of some of the choices well-meaning Christian parents allow their children to make—as if they (the parents) had no say in the matter. They permit their children to have unsupervised relationships with peers who do not have a heart for God; to date non-Christians; to be disrespectful and sullen; to dress inappropriately; and to be entertained by worldly music, television, movies, and videos—and then wonder why their children love the world and resent Christianity.

Some time ago, I was asked to speak to the faculty and staff of a large Christian school. The staff member who issued the invitation expressed her concern for the spiritual condition of the students. She said to me, "The kids in this school hate God; they hate the Bible. They have no interest in spiritual matters." If that is the case, we must be honest enough to ask ourselves: What have those young people seen (or not seen) in their homes that has produced this result?

Thankfully, there are some notable exceptions in Generation X. But my experience in observing church youth groups across the country leads me to believe that a majority of young people growing up in "Christian homes" have little or no appetite for the things of God.

The Truth is that there is something wrong in us—our generation of Christian adults—when our children are growing up not wanting to have anything to do with God or, worse yet, claiming to be Christians while living in a way that is contrary to the Word of God. That doesn't mean that every godly parent will have only godly children; but when we have this widespread epidemic of young men and women growing up in Christian homes and rejecting what their parents supposedly stood for, we have to admit that something is missing in that generation of parents.

If we persist in believing the lie that we are not responsible for our children, we play into the hands of the Enemy, who is determined to claim the next generation for his kingdom. The Scripture teaches that each generation is responsible to pass on to the next a heritage of godliness. This is both an awesome privilege and a weighty responsibility. The sobering fact is that we are responsible for the seeds we sow, and we must live with the harvest that results. We cannot plant seeds of halfhearted, undisciplined, worldly lives, and then hope for a "crop failure" in the next generation.

Of course, the balancing biblical Truth is that each generation is responsible for its own walk and obedience. Regardless of what their parents have or have not done right, each individual will one day give account to God for his or her own choices (Deuteronomy 24:16; Jeremiah 31:29–30).

Being a parent is a high and holy calling. There is no more demanding occupation. The best of parents are utterly dependent on the Holy Spirit to make it "click" with their children. That is why a mother's greatest human resource is prayer.

The Enemy lies to parents in an effort to sabotage the relay of Truth from one generation to the next. Parents who believe and act on his lies will place themselves and their children in bondage. But parents who believe and act on the Truth will be set free to love, enjoy, train, and nurture their children and, by God's grace, to send those children out to reflect God's glory and grace to the next generation.

THE LIE	THE TRUTH
27. IT'S UP TO US TO DETERMINE THE SIZE OF OUR FAMILY.	• God is the Creator and Giver of life. • Anything that hinders or discourages women from fulfilling their God-given calling to be bearers and nurturers of life furthers Satan's schemes and aids his efforts. • One of the purposes of marriage is to produce a "godly offspring." • Childbearing is a basic, God-given role for women. Children are to be received as a blessing from God.
28. CHILDREN NEED TO GET EXPOSED TO THE "REAL WORLD" SO THAT THEY CAN LEARN TO FUNCTION IN IT.	• Our task is not to raise up children who can fit into this world or merely survive it but to bring up children who will be used by God to change our world. • Like young, tender plants, children need to be protected from worldly influences until they are spiritually mature enough to withstand them. • The fear of the Lord and a vital, personal relationship with God are the best means of preparing children to withstand secular culture and to make a difference in our world.
29. ALL CHILDREN WILL GO THROUGH A REBELLIOUS STAGE.	• If parents expect their children to rebel, they increase the likelihood that they will do so. • God promises a blessing to parents who keep His covenant and who teach their children to do the same.

THE LIE	THE TRUTH
	• Parents cannot force their children to walk with God, but they can model godliness and cultivate a climate in the home that creates an appetite for God and is conducive to the spiritual nurture and growth of their children.
30. I KNOW MY CHILD IS A CHRISTIAN BECAUSE HE PRAYED TO RECEIVE CHRIST AT AN EARLY AGE.	• Those who do not have a heart for God or any hunger for the things of God and who have a consistent pattern of rejecting the Word and ways of God have no basis for assurance of salvation. • Parents who assume their children know the Lord, regardless of their lifestyle, may give their children a false sense of security and may not be praying appropriately for their children.
31. WE ARE NOT RESPONSIBLE FOR HOW OUR CHILDREN TURN OUT.	• Parents have enormous influence in molding the lives of their children by their example, their teaching, and their leadership. • Each generation is responsible to pass on to the next the heritage of a heart that knows and walks with God. • Parents will give account to God for the spiritual condition of the lives He has entrusted to their care. • Each individual is responsible for his own walk and obedience. Regardless of what kind of parents he had, each person will give account to God for his own choices.

1. AGREE with God.

What lies have you believed about parenting and children?

_____

_____

2. ACCEPT responsibility.

How has believing those lies manifested itself in the way you live (e.g., attitudes, actions)?

_____

_____

3. AFFIRM the Truth.

Read aloud each of the Truths listed on pages 188–89. Which of these Truths do you particularly need to embrace at this time?

_____

Renew your mind (your thinking) by the Word of God. Read the following passages aloud. What do these verses reveal about God's perspective on children and parenting?

Psalm 127

_____

Matthew 19:13–15

_____

Psalm 78:1–8

_____

1 Thessalonians 2:7

_____

4. ACT on the Truth.

What specific step(s) of action do you need to take to align your life with the Truth?

_____

_____

5. ASK God to help you walk in the Truth.

Thank You for Your Father's heart, dear Lord. Thank You for making me Your child through faith in Christ and for the way You care for me, meet my needs, and work to bring me to spiritual maturity. Thank You for Your love for children; help me to receive and love them as You do. Thank You for designing me as a woman to be a bearer and nurturer of life. Please show me how to fulfill my calling as a mother—whether of my own physical children or of spiritual children You give to me. Help me to faithfully nurture those You have entrusted to my care. May my life create in the next generation a hunger and thirst for righteousness and a longing to be like their heavenly Father. In Jesus' name. Amen

CHAPTER EIGHT

LIES WOMEN BELIEVE... ABOUT EMOTIONS

Dear diary,

It's been nearly two years since we lost Abel; I think about him all the time—it still hurts so much. We haven't heard anything from Cain for months. Sometimes I feel so angry toward him for what he did to us; other times I just want to hold him and rock him and sing to him like I did when he was a baby.

Adam won't talk about how he feels—sometimes I wonder if he feels anything at all. It seems to annoy him when I try to get him to understand how I feel.

I just can't seem to dig out of this empty, lonely hole. Some days I can hardly drag myself out of bed. I feel like the darkness is about to swallow me up. I don't know how much longer I can hang on. I can't remember what it was like not to hurt. Will I ever be happy again?

At a ladies' conference I attended some years ago, we were given a magnet with a list of words describing a variety of emotions—words such as *confused, ecstatic, angry, frustrated, sad, confident, happy, lonely,* and *depressed.* Above each word was a humorous line drawing of a face depicting that particular feeling.

The list came with a smaller magnet in the shape of a frame that said, "Today I Feel . . ." This piece was designed to be placed over any one of the cartoon drawings to express "how I am feeling today."

If some of us changed the marker every time our emotions changed, we would be kept quite busy. In fact, many women feel most of those emotions at least once a month! More than anything else, it is probably our female emotional makeup that sometimes causes men to throw up their hands and say, "I give up. I just can't figure you out!" And, in a sense, who can blame them?

When we wrestle with out-of-control emotions, it is easy to conclude that emotions are inherently sinful or wrong and should be suppressed. We need to remember that being created in the image of God means we have the capacity to experience and express a variety of emotions. God exhibits a spectrum of pure emotions, including joy, delight, anger, jealousy, and sorrow. And He has designed us to be able to feel and express many different emotions in a way that reflects His heart and brings glory to Him.

The problem is not that we *have* emotions—they are a gift from God. The problem is that our emotions (unlike God's) are tainted by the Fall. The challenge is to let the Spirit of God sanctify us in the realm of our emotions so that they can be expressed in godly ways.

I know of no tool that the Enemy uses more effectively to lead us as women into bondage than our emotions. He does so by causing us to believe things about our emotions that just aren't true.

🍎 32. "IF I FEEL SOMETHING, IT MUST BE TRUE."

The Enemy wants us to believe that if we *feel* unloved, we *are* unloved. If we *feel* we can't cope with the pressure, it must be true that

194

we can't make it. If we *feel* God has deserted us or that He has acted unjustly in a matter that concerns us, then perhaps He has let us down. If we *feel* our situation is hopeless, then there must be no hope. If we don't *feel* saved, then maybe we aren't. If we don't *feel* forgiven, then we must not be.

The Truth is that, due to our fallen condition, our feelings often have very little to do with reality. In many instances, feelings are simply not a reliable gauge of what is actually true. When we allow them to be tied to our circumstances—which are constantly changing—rather than to the unchangeable realities of God and His Truth, our emotions are prone to fluctuate wildly.

It doesn't take much to put our emotions on an upswing—a clear, sunny day, a raise at work, a compliment from a friend, the successful completion of a big project, or losing five pounds. Meanwhile, emotional lows can be the result of a variety of factors including (but not limited to) a series of cloudy days, a tough day at the office, a disappointing phone call, the realization that our clothes have gotten too tight, the time of the month, a sleepless night, or a pizza we ate too late the night before.

When you add in "big" things like the birth of a fourth child in five years, a major move, the loss of a job, the death of a mate or child, caring for a parent with Alzheimer's, going through the change of life, or being diagnosed with cancer, those emotions can really go haywire.

In the midst of the roller coaster ride our emotions sometimes take us on, we have to constantly bring our minds and thoughts back to the Truth. The Truth is, God is good, whether I feel like He is good or not. The Truth is, God loves me, whether I feel loved or not. The Truth is, through faith in the shed blood of Jesus Christ on my behalf, I am forgiven, whether I feel forgiven or not. The Truth is, God will never leave me or forsake me; He is with me all the time, even when I feel alone and forsaken.

If we want to walk in freedom, we must realize that our emotions are not necessarily trustworthy and be willing to reject any feelings that are not consistent with the Truth.

"Connie" acknowledges having based her beliefs on what she felt, rather than on the Truth. Notice how her whole way of thinking changed once she realized she could let the Truth rule over her feelings:

❧ ☙

Although I was a child of God, I had believed throughout my life that certain aspects of the Truth applied to everyone except me. God was good to them, not to me. God loved them, not me. Others were of great worth to God, but not me. I knew the "facts"—that God is good, He loves me, and I am of great worth to Him; but there was a disconnection in my mind between the facts and how I felt. Surely, if God loved me and I meant so much to Him, I would feel loved and valuable.

Through your seminar on "Lies Women Believe," God revealed that His Truth stands, regardless of how I feel. Nothing can change God or the Truth of His Word and His character. He is good to me. He does love me. I can choose to cling to the Truth or I can choose to buy into the lies of Satan. But God's Truth is unchangeable and irrefutable.

❧ ☙

In the last chapter of Philippians, the apostle Paul gives a prescription for mental sanity and emotional stability:

> Rejoice in the Lord always. . . . Do not be anxious about anything, but in everything, by prayer and petition, with thanksgiving, present your requests to God. . . . Whatever is true . . . think about such things.

The result?

The peace of God, which transcends all understanding,
will guard your hearts and your minds in Christ Jesus. . . .
And the God of peace will be with you.

Philippians 4:4, 6–9

33. "I CAN'T CONTROL MY EMOTIONS."

The Enemy uses this lie to make us believe we have no choice but to be controlled by our emotions. While it may be true to some degree that we can't help the way we feel, the Truth is that we don't have to let our feelings run our lives.

You may not be able to help feeling apprehensive about an upcoming medical exam, but that doesn't mean you can't stop worrying and fretting about the outcome. You may not be able to help feeling edgy or irritable at a certain time of the month, but that doesn't mean you can't help speaking "rudely" to or acting roughly toward whoever happens to get in your way on those days. You may not be able to help feeling vulnerable in a lonely season of your life when a married man takes an interest in you, but that doesn't mean you can't help "falling in love" with him.

The Truth is, regardless of what emotions are whirling around inside, by God's grace, we can choose to fix our minds on Him and to "trust and obey." When we do, we will experience His peace and the grace to be faithful, even though our circumstances may not change.

The much-loved author Hannah Whitall Smith was plagued with circumstances that could have left her an emotional basket case. She was married to a preacher who proved to be spiritually and emotionally unstable and who was repeatedly unfaithful. Two of her five children died of scarlet fever. One daughter abandoned her husband and ran off with an artist; another daughter married an outspoken atheist. Hannah herself suffered from painful arthritis. But she refused to let her life be dictated by feelings. Her writings reflect her stead-fast determination to exercise her will in obedience to God, regard-less of her emotions.

> We must choose, without any regard to the state of our emotions, what attitude our will will take toward God. We must recognize that our emotions are only the servants of our will. . . .
>
> Our will can control our feelings if only we are steadfastly minded to do so. Many times when my feelings have declared contrary to the facts, I have changed those feelings entirely by a steadfast assertion of their opposite. . . .
>
> Surging emotions—like a tossing vessel, which by degrees yields to the steady pull of the anchor—finding themselves attached to the mighty power of God by the choice of your will, must sooner or later give allegiance to Him.[1]

The Scripture is filled with divine promises and commands that provide the means by which our emotions may be steadied in the midst of any storm:

- God's Word promises, "I am with you always" (Matthew 28:20). Therefore, we don't have to be overcome by loneliness.
- God's Word promises, "My God will meet all your needs" (Philippians 4:19). Therefore, we don't have to stay awake at night worrying about how the mortgage will get paid.
- God's Word promises, "Though the mountains be shaken and the hills be removed, yet my unfailing love for you will not be shaken" (Isaiah 54:10). Therefore, we don't have to live in dread of an uncertain future.
- God's Word says, "Do not be afraid" (John 14:27). That means we don't have to give in to fear, regardless of our circumstances.
- God's Word says, "Don't worry about anything" (Philippians

4:6 TLB). That means that even in the midst of stressful circumstances, we don't have to be anxious.

- God's Word says, "Give thanks in all circumstances" (1 Thessalonians 5:18). That means we can choose to be thankful, even
when everything around us seems to be falling apart.

- God's Word says, "Love your enemies" (Matthew 5:44). That
means, by the power of the Spirit, we can choose to love anyone—no matter how greatly they have wronged us.

- God's Word says, "If you hold anything against anyone, forgive
him" (Mark 11:25). That means there is no one we cannot
choose to forgive, no matter how deeply they may have hurt
us or sinned against us.

When we fix our minds on Christ and bring every thought into
subjection to the Truth, the Holy Spirit sanctifies our emotions and
grants supernatural grace, comfort, and peace:

Since, then, you have been raised with Christ,
set your hearts on things above, where Christ is
seated at the right hand of God. Set your minds
on things above, not on earthly things.

Colossians 3:1–2

We take captive every thought to
make it obedient to Christ.

2 Corinthians 10:5b

Thou wilt keep him in perfect peace, whose mind
is stayed on thee: because he trusteth in thee.

Isaiah 26:3 KJV

199

34. "I CAN'T HELP HOW I RESPOND WHEN MY HORMONES ARE OUT OF WHACK. (IT'S UNDERSTANDABLE TO ACT LIKE A SHREW AT CERTAIN TIMES.)"

If we accept the lie that we can't control our emotions, we will also believe we can't control how we act when we are feeling emotionally vulnerable or out of control. Not only are we too quick to *believe* our feelings, we are also far too quick to *obey* them.

So if we feel a sudden craving for a big bowl of chocolate ice cream at ten o'clock at night, we head for the freezer and pull out the ice cream. If we feel like staying up and watching a late-night movie, we do so. If we don't feel like getting out of bed the next morning, we pull the covers up over our head and call in sick at work. If we don't feel like cooking a meal that night, we call for pizza delivery. If we don't feel like cleaning our house, we let it go until the mess is so great we are *really* depressed.

The problem is, if we cater to our emotions and let them control our actions in these kinds of daily routines, we will be more vulnerable to being controlled by our emotions in the major transitions and difficult seasons of life.

In recent decades, there has been a lot of research, writing, and discussion regarding the seasons of a woman's life. Some of this focus has increased our understanding of the way that we are "fearfully and wonderfully made." However, it has also caused many women to become obsessed with themselves and provided them with an excuse for inexcusable attitudes and behavior.

Some women I know habitually attribute their negative moods and reactions to where they are in their monthly cycle (as I am frequently tempted to do myself). This way of thinking almost cost "Marie" her marriage:

❦

I am fifty-two years old, and I can see how this lie had my heart completely deceived. My husband tried to confront me and help me

see the Truth, but I was so deceived and reinforced by the PMS
proponents that there was no way I would listen. I had to face the
possibility of my husband leaving before my eyes were opened.

❧ ❦

For some women, a difficult pregnancy "explains" (read *justifies*)
erratic mood swings and volatile behavior. I have met other women
who seem to be planning ahead to have a breakdown when they hit
menopause.

Certainly what happens in our bodies does affect us emotionally, mentally, and even spiritually. We cannot isolate these various di-
mensions of who we are—they are inseparably intertwined. But we
fall into the trap of the Enemy when we justify fleshly, sinful attitudes and responses based on our physical condition or hormonal
changes.

My recollection of the year I was twelve is that I cried the whole
year—for no apparent reason. As I look back on it, I understand better now than I did then some of the changes that were taking place
in my body as I was becoming a woman. But I also understand better now than I did then that what was happening in my body was
no excuse for the moodiness and mouthiness that were part of my
pattern during that year.

I remember an occasion years ago when I was physically and emotionally wrung out from an intense speaking schedule. My attitude
and my tongue were on a roll; I was being negative and generally hard
to live with. Subconsciously I was justifying myself because of how
I was feeling. A friend who happened to be within the radius of my
cantankerous spirit looked at me and said simply, "Don't let tiredness be an excuse for carnality." I confess that at the moment, I didn't
particularly appreciate the rebuke, but it was exactly what I needed
to hear—a painful, but necessary, reminder of the Truth.

As with other aspects of nature, God has designed our bodies to
function in seasons and cycles. Certainly each season of life has its
challenges. One of the consequences of the Fall was that childbearing
would be accompanied by sorrow and pain. Childbirth is not the only

time those consequences are felt. For example, the difficulties some women experience associated with their menstrual cycle are a practical reminder of our fallen condition.

But every monthly cycle is also a reminder that God made us *women,* and that with our womanhood comes the capacity for being a bearer and nurturer of life. Even as a single woman, I find this to be a gracious and valuable reminder of who I am, why God created me, and how I can best glorify Him here on this earth.

Didn't God make our bodies? Doesn't He understand how they work? Do you think things like menstrual cycles, hormones, pregnancy, and menopause catch Him off guard?

The psalmist praises God for His watch care and His sovereign plan as it relates to the creation of our physical bodies:

> You created my inmost being;
> you knit me together in my mother's womb.
> I praise you because I am fearfully
> and wonderfully made. . . .
> When I was woven together in the depths of the earth,
> your eyes saw my unformed body.
> All the days ordained for me
> were written in your book
> before one of them came to be.

Psalm 139:13–16

What an incredible thought! Long before you were born, every molecule of your body and every day of your life, from conception to the grave, was carefully thought through and planned by God. He ordained the day you would start menstruation, when and how many times you would be able to conceive, and exactly when you would stop ovulating. He understands exactly what is taking place in your body through every season and change.

Is it conceivable that this wise, loving Creator would be unaware of our hormone levels at any stage of maturity or would have failed to make provision for every season of life? He does not offer an easy or trouble-free process of growth. But He has promised to meet all our needs and to give us grace to respond to the challenges and difficulties associated with every stage of life.

Long before anyone had ever written a book on the subject of menopause or estrogen, Francis de Sales (1567–1622) wrote words of wise counsel for women of every generation:

> Do not look forward to the changes and chances of this life in fear; rather look to them with full hope that, as they arise, God, whose you are, will deliver you out of them. He has kept you hitherto,—do you but hold fast to His dear hand, and He will lead you safely through all things; and, when you cannot stand, He will bear you in His arms. ...The same everlasting Father who cares for you today, will take care of you to-morrow, and every day. Either He will shield you from suffering, or He will give you unfailing strength to bear it. Be at peace then, and put aside all anxious thoughts and imaginations.[2]

Paul's prayer at the end of his first letter to the Thessalonians is not just for first-century believers. And it is not just for men. I believe it is a prayer that can be claimed by women in every season of their lives. It is a prayer we can expect God to answer, as we exercise faith and allow Him to do so:

May God himself, the God of peace, sanctify you through
and through. May your whole spirit, soul
[including those emotions!] and body be kept blameless at
the coming of our Lord Jesus Christ. The one
who calls you is faithful and he will do it.

1 Thessalonians 5:23–24

🍎 35. "THE ANSWER TO DEPRESSION MUST FIRST BE SOUGHT IN MEDICATION AND/OR PSYCHOTHERAPY."

As I was writing this chapter, I received a call from a pastor's wife. She poured out her heart about a battle of many years that her husband has had with depression. The effects in her life and in their marriage have been significant.

During the course of the conversation, she asked the kinds of questions that many ask in similar circumstances: Could this be a genetic problem? (There is suicide in her husband's family background.) Could it be something organic or chemical? Could some kind of demonic activity be involved? Is there some spiritual truth he is not grasping that accounts for the turmoil and bondage?

Depression is a particularly major issue for women—twice as many women as men suffer from depression. Never before has there been such widespread depression among women as what we are experiencing today in the West. In spite of how readily physicians diagnose depression and treat it with psychotherapy and drugs, the number of sufferers is only growing, and relatively few people are finding lasting relief.

A study of depression and despair in the Scripture reveals that, in some cases, the pain we identify as emotional depression is simply one of the unavoidable consequences of living in a fallen world. In Romans 8, Paul indicates that the entire creation "groans" under the weight of its fallen condition, longing for our final redemption from this sin-cursed world.

Much scientific and medical research has been done to try to understand the interrelationship between depression, genetic predispositions, and other physiological factors. We still have much to learn about these matters and about the long-term effects of various types of treatment. What we do know is that in many cases, physiological symptoms connected with depression are the fruit of issues that are rooted in the realm of the soul and spirit—issues such as ingratitude, unresolved conflict, irresponsibility, guilt, bitterness, unforgiveness, un-belief, claiming of rights, anger, and self-centeredness.

If these root issues are not addressed God's way, the consequences will inevitably show up in our bodies and souls, creating very real physical and emotional problems. In some instances, medication may help to alleviate the symptoms of depression. However, if the de-pression originated in something other than a physical malfunction, medication will not permanently solve the problem. Properly ad-ministered, medication may help a severely depressed person get sta-bilized enough to think clearly, providing a window of opportunity for the individual to begin dealing with the issues that created the problem. But there is no prescription drug that can "fix" the deeper issues of the spirit. Unfortunately, far too many people suffering from depression have come to view medication as a "solution" for their problem. If the sufferer does not address those inner heart issues, she cannot hope to ever be truly free.

You may be surprised to learn that numerous individuals in the Bible suffered with what we would call today depressive illnesses. Their stories provide helpful insight into some of the contributing causes of depression.

For example, King Ahab became depressed when he couldn't get his own way. When Ahab's neighbor refused to sell him a piece of property he badly wanted, he threw a temper tantrum— he became "sullen and angry. . . . He lay on his bed sulking and refused to eat" (1 Kings 21:4). Ahab's wife, Jezebel, attempted to pull him out of his depression by promising to help him get what he wanted. She said to him, "Get up and eat! Cheer up. I'll get you the vineyard of Naboth the Jezreelite" (1 Kings 21:7).

In my own life, I have had to admit that my emotional lows are generally the result of my reaction to things not going "my way." Deep down, I am angry—but rather than express that anger outwardly, I sink into an emotional pit, hoping that someone will notice and at-tempt to make me feel better, even as Jezebel did to Ahab.

The story of Jonah illustrates how depression and suicidal thoughts can be rooted in anger against God's choices. When God did not destroy the Ninevites as Jonah felt they deserved, "Jonah was greatly displeased and became angry. He prayed to the LORD, '...Now, O LORD, take away my life, for it is better for me to die than to live'" (Jonah 4:1–3). God's response forced Jonah to face up to his anger: "But the LORD replied, 'Have you any right to be angry?'" (4:4). The same exchange was repeated a short time later, when Jonah became further depressed after a vine that had provided shade withered up and died. God wanted the prophet to see that it was not his circumstances that were actually causing his depression; rather, it was his angry response to God's sovereign choices.

Hannah was a godly woman who became depressed when she had to deal with a combination of unfulfilled longings and a strained relationship over a prolonged period of time. She had a godly husband who loved her dearly. However, for reasons known only to the Lord, He had closed her womb. Hannah's struggles with barrenness were exacerbated by her husband's other wife, Peninnah, who had no difficulty conceiving and bearing children and didn't hesitate to remind Hannah of that fact:

> Her rival kept provoking her in order to irritate her.
> This went on year after year. Whenever Hannah
> went up to the house of the LORD, her rival
> provoked her till she wept and would not eat.
>
> *1 Samuel 1:6–7*

When we fail to see God's hand in our circumstances or when we contend with Him over His choices for our lives, we become candidates for emotional and spiritual depression.

King David's life illustrates that sometimes depression is caused by our own sin, while at other times it is simply the pain caused by living in this fallen world.

Psalm 32 relates the physical and emotional anguish that resulted when he refused to confess his sin in the matter of Bathsheba and Uriah:

When I kept silent about my sin, my body wasted away
through my groaning all day long.
For day and night Your hand was heavy upon me;
My vitality was drained away as with the fever heat of summer.

Psalm 32:3–4 NASB

In contrast to the depression he experienced because of his sin, David periodically encountered times of intense emotional darkness that were not directly connected to his own sin. A number of the psalms express the depths of his despair:

My thoughts trouble me and I am distraught....
My heart is in anguish within me;
the terrors of death assail me.
Fear and trembling have beset me;
horror has overwhelmed me....
My tears have been my food day and night....

Psalms 55:2, 4–5; 42:3a

Through such seasons, David learned how to let God reach him in his lowest points. He understood the necessity of speaking truth to himself, asking himself the tough questions, and counseling his heart according to the Truth of God's character.

Why art thou cast down, O my soul? and why art thou disquieted in me? hope thou in God: for I shall yet praise him
for the help of his countenance. O my God, my soul is cast
down within me: therefore will I remember thee....
The LORD will command his lovingkindness in
the daytime, and in the night his song shall be with me.

Psalm 42:5–6, 8 KJV

In his classic book, *Spiritual Depression,* Dr. Martyn Lloyd-Jones uses this passage to address those who are depressed:

You must say to your soul, "Why art thou cast down"—what business have you to be disquieted? You must . . . exhort yourself, and say to yourself: "Hope thou in God"—instead of muttering in this depressed, unhappy way. And then you must go on to remind yourself of God, Who God is, and what God is and what God has done, and what God has pledged Himself to do.[3]

In the last chapter of the book of James, we discover a passage that provides practical help for those who are struggling with depression:

Is any among you afflicted? let him pray. Is any merry?
let him sing psalms. Is any sick among you? let him call
for the elders of the church; and let them pray
over him, anointing him with oil in the name of
the Lord: and the prayer of faith shall save the sick,
and the Lord shall raise him up; and if he hath
committed sins, they shall be forgiven him.
Confess your faults one to another, and pray one
for another, that ye may be healed. The effectual fervent
prayer of a righteous man availeth much.

James 5:13–16 KJV

The first Truth that stands out in this passage is that regardless of how we are feeling or what we are going through, our immediate response should be to turn to the Lord. Whether we are prospering or suffering, happy or sad, healthy or sick—before we do anything else, we should acknowledge God's presence and ask Him to walk with us through the experience, to direct us in responding to the circumstances, and to provide His resources to deal with the situation.

More often than not, it seems our first response is to turn to some-one or something other than the Lord. When we are hurting, we are quick to turn to tangible resources in search of comfort, relief, or escape. After all, it is a lot easier to call a friend for sympathy than to get on our knees with an open Bible and listen to what God wants to say to us in the "dark night of our soul." It is a lot easier to try to mask the pain with excessive food or sleep than to choose to deny our flesh and walk in the Spirit. It is easier to drown out our feel-ings with the blare of the television than to humble ourselves and seek forgiveness from God and others for our anger. It is easier to pay for a refill of Prozac than to ask God to show us if we have an ungrate-ful, demanding, or bitter spirit. These means may provide a measure of relief, but they are likely to be inadequate and short-lived. Noth-ing less than the "God of all comfort" can meet our deepest needs at such times.

This is not to say that all those other things are wrong. A good night's sleep can make a lot of difference in how a mother with two preschoolers and a newborn feels. Sometimes a change in diet can greatly affect our physical well-being, which in turn affects our emo-tional and mental well being. Physical exercise can be tremendously beneficial in dealing with physical symptoms related to depression. Friends can provide encouragement, especially if they help point our thinking back to the Truth. A physician may be able to detect and help correct a physical problem that is impacting our emotional con-dition. But our tendency to look to professionals and pills to solve what, in many cases, are problems of the soul and spirit has left mil-lions of women overmedicated, financially broke, disillusioned, and no better off than when they started.

The second Truth James emphasizes is the importance and role of the body of Christ in ministering help and healing to hurting hearts.

In the last several decades, we have developed a mind-set that only "professionals" are qualified to help people who are plagued with various emotional or mental disorders. Even many pastors have been made to feel incompetent to deal with these issues and therefore routinely refer troubled counselees to "the experts"—professionally trained psychologists, psychiatrists, or therapists.

I am not suggesting that there is no place for people who have been trained in these fields, if their counsel is rooted in the Word and ways of God. However, let's not forget that God has placed within the body of Christ the resources to minister to desperate, needy people. He has given us His Word and His Spirit. We need to learn how to take the ointment of the Word of God and apply it to the needs of hurting people in the body of Christ.

And so, James says, when you are hurting, when your soul is sick, let the body of Christ minister grace in the name of Jesus. After you have first prayed yourself, then take the initiative to share your needs with "one another"—particularly with your spiritual leaders; ask them to pray for you. Confess any sin that may be causing emotional weakness or sickness in your life, and be willing to be accountable to the body through the process of healing and restoration.

When it comes to dealing with our emotions, we must remember that "feeling good" is not the ultimate objective in the Christian's life. God does not promise that those who walk with Him will be free from all difficult emotions. In fact, as long as we are in these bodies, we will experience varying degrees of pain and distress.

As we will see in the next chapter, the real focus of our lives must not be on changing or "fixing" things to make ourselves feel better but on the glory of God and His redemptive purposes in the world. Everything else is expendable. True joy comes from abandoning ourselves to that end.

THE LIE	THE TRUTH
32. IF I FEEL SOMETHING, IT MUST BE TRUE.	• My feelings cannot always be trusted. They often have little to do with reality and can easily deceive me into believing things that are not true. • I must choose to reject any feelings that are not consistent with the Truth.
33. I CAN'T CONTROL MY EMOTIONS.	• I do not have to be controlled by my emotions. • I can choose to fix my mind on the Truth, to take every thought captive to the Truth, and to let God control my emotions.
34. I CAN'T HELP HOW I RESPOND WHEN MY HORMONES ARE OUT OF WHACK.	• By God's grace, I can choose to obey Him regardless of how I feel. • There is no excuse for ungodly attitudes, responses, or behavior. • My physical and emotional cycles and seasons are under the control of the One who made me, cares for me, and has made provision for each stage of my life.
35. THE ANSWER TO DEPRESSION MUST FIRST BE SOUGHT IN MEDICATION AND/OR PSYCHOTHERAPY.	• Physical and emotional symptoms of depression may be the fruit of issues in the spirit that need to be addressed. • If my depression did not originate as a physical problem, medication will not permanently relieve my depression. • I do not have a "right" to "feel good." Regardless of how I feel, I can choose to give thanks, to obey God, and to reach out to others. • God has given us powerful resources—His grace, His Spirit, His Word, His promises, the body of Christ—to minister to our emotional needs.

1. AGREE with God.

What lies have you believed about your emotions?

_____

_____

2. ACCEPT responsibility.

How has believing those lies manifested itself in the way you live (e.g., attitudes, actions)?

_____

_____

3. AFFIRM the Truth.

Read aloud each of the Truths listed on page 211. Which of these Truths do you particularly need to embrace at this time?

_____

Renew your mind (your thinking) by the Word of God. Read the following passages aloud. What do these verses reveal about how to deal with our emotions?

Philippians 4:4–8

_____

Colossians 3:1–4

_____

Isaiah 26:3–4

_____

Isaiah 50:10

_____

4. ACT on the Truth.

What specific step(s) of action do you need to take to align your life with the Truth?

_____

_____

5. ASK God to help you walk in the Truth.

Thank You, Father, for the gift of emotions—for allowing us to experience joy and delight in what is good and even for the ability to experience pain. I acknowledge that in this fallen world pain is an inescapable reality. I confess that I often choose to believe and act on my feelings without stopping to consider whether or not those feelings are based on Truth. I frequently allow my responses to be controlled by how I am feeling and by my circumstances, rather than by Your Word and Your Spirit. Thank You that, regardless of how I feel or what my emotions tell me, Your Truth is absolute and unchanging. Help me to trust You even in the midst of tears, pain, confusion, or loss, and to obey You, regardless of how I feel. Thank You for the peace You have promised, in the midst of any circumstance, if I will fix my heart and thoughts on You. In Jesus' name. Amen.

CHAPTER NINE

LIES WOMEN BELIEVE...ABOUT CIRCUMSTANCES

Dear diary,

What a year it has been! We received word that one of Cain's grandsons had a bad fall while working on a building project for his dad. Apparently he was pretty seriously injured. It's been hard to find out a lot of details, since we have so little communication with Cain and his family. That whole relationship is still very strained and the memories so painful at times.

This year's harvest has been the poorest I can remember. Adam has had to work a lot of extra hours just to get enough food for us to survive. By the time he gets home at the end of the day, he's exhausted and doesn't feel like talking or doing much of anything.

I wish I could say I've been an encourager to him through all this, but I've had my own struggles—I just don't have the energy I used to have, and I often feel overwhelmed trying to keep up with things around the house, especially with four children still at home.

Our lives are so hectic—it's hard to know how to juggle a hus-
band, children, grandchildren, and housework, and still find time
for myself.

Sometimes the pressure really gets to me and I find myself be-
ing out of sorts with everything and everyone around me. I feel bad
about the way I take things out on the kids and Adam. I'm just so
tired.

It's been so long since Adam and I have had time together—
just the two of us. I wish we could find a way to get away from it
all for a while. Maybe that would help me cope better. I know
something's got to change.

It was "one of those days." You've had them—you know, when
nothing goes right. You may have read about this particular day in
Alexander and the Terrible, Horrible, No Good, Very Bad Day by Judith Viorst.
It seemed that everything was going wrong for poor Alexander.

I went to sleep with gum in my mouth and now there's gum in
my hair and when I got out of bed this morning I tripped on the
skateboard and by mistake I dropped my sweater in the sink while the
water was running and I could tell it was going to be a terrible, horrible, no good, very bad day.[1]

And he was right. Alexander had a horrible day at school, a no-
good dentist appointment, and a very bad stop at the shoe store. And
that wasn't the end of it.

There were lima beans for dinner and I hate limas.
There was kissing on TV and I hate kissing.
My bath was too hot, I got soap in my eyes, my marble went down
the drain, and I had to wear my railroad-train pajamas. I hate my railroad-
train pajamas.
When I went to bed Nick took back the pillow he said I could keep
and the Mickey Mouse night light burned out and I bit my tongue.

The cat wants to sleep with Anthony, not with me.
It has been a terrible, horrible, no good, very bad day.[2]

Who can blame the frustrated boy for sighing at the end of the day, "I think I'll move to Australia!"[3]

Alexander isn't the only one who has felt that way. We've probably all had times when we wished God would call us to the uninhabited regions of the earth!

In fact, that is exactly what the psalmist prayed on at least one occasion. Everything seemed to be pressing in on him, and apparently he felt he had had about all he could take:

> I said, "Oh, that I had the wings of a dove!
> I would fly away and be at rest ...
> I would hurry to my place of shelter,
> far from the tempest and storm."

Psalm 55:6, 8

When God first created the earth, He looked at everything He had made and said, "It is good." From the tiniest molecule to the most expansive galaxy in the universe, everything was in perfect order. All existed in perfect harmony. There was no such thing as confusion or heartache or conflict or frustration.

As we have seen, Adam and Eve enjoyed a perfect environment. Their first home would have made Martha Stewart envious. Everything worked. Nothing was broken or needed to be fixed. No one was ever late or tired or irritable. No one ever got into debt or had a headache or got sick or died. No one ever got his feelings hurt or said something insensitive or sued anybody. There was no need for therapists or lawyers or doctors or Dr. Laura.

But all that changed the instant Eve listened to and acted on Satan's lie. Where once the ground had readily yielded food for the man and woman to eat, now the man had to contend with thorns and thistles to provide for his family. Giving birth was intended to be a joyous, natural experience for the woman; now she had to endure labor and pain in childbirth.

In addition to thorns and labor pains, the fallen, human experience would include

fear, shame, and guilt	*hurricanes, floods, and earthquakes*
disappointment	*crime and violence*
arguments and lawsuits	*poverty, starvation, racism, and war*
tears and temper tantrums	*arthritis, tumors, and cancer*

The entrance of deception into the world had far-reaching consequences. Like a drop of food coloring poured into a glass of water, sin tainted everything about human beings and their environment.

Most people live with unnecessary disappointment, anger, and despair because they have been deceived in relation to their circumstances and the suffering that is inevitable in this fallen world.

36. "IF MY CIRCUMSTANCES WERE DIFFERENT, *I* WOULD BE DIFFERENT."

I remember talking years ago with a young mother who had a two-year-old child and one-year-old twins. She said with a sigh, "I was never an impatient person—until I had these twins!" This lady believed what most of us have believed at one time or another—that we are the way we are because of our circumstances.

The implication is that our circumstances make us what we are. Perhaps you've found yourself saying, as have I, "She made me *so* mad!" What we are saying is: "I am really a kind, gentle, loving, self-controlled, Spirit-filled woman. *But* . . . you can't believe what she did . . . !"

"I wouldn't have lost my cool," we insist, "if my child hadn't filled the dryer with water and painted the living room furniture with butter!"

Or, "I wouldn't struggle in my marriage, if my parents hadn't verbally abused me and made me feel worthless."

Or, "I wouldn't be so bitter, if my husband hadn't run off with that other woman."

We are saying, "Someone or something made me the way I am." We feel that if our circumstances were different—our upbringing, our environment, the people around us—we would be different. We would be more patient, more loving, more content, easier to live with.

If our circumstances make us what we are, then we are all victims. And that's just what the Enemy wants us to believe. Because if we are victims, then we aren't responsible—we can't help the way we are. But God says we *are* responsible—not for the failures of others, but for our own responses and lives.

The Truth is, our circumstances do not make us what we are. They merely reveal what we are. That exasperated mother who believed she had never been an impatient person until she had twins did not understand that she had always been an impatient person; she just didn't realize how impatient she was until God brought a set of circumstances into her life to show her what she was really like—so He could change her.

The Enemy convinces us that the only way we can ever be different is if our circumstances change. So we play the "if only" game:

If only we didn't have to move . . .
If only we lived closer to my parents . . .
If only we had a bigger house (more closets, more storage) . . .
If only we had more money . . .
If only my husband didn't have to work so many hours . . .
If only I were married . . .
If only I weren't married . . .
If only I were married to someone different . . .
If only I had children . . .
If only I didn't have so many children . . .
If only I hadn't lost that child . . .

If only my husband would communicate . . .
If only my husband were a spiritual leader . . .

We have been deceived into believing we would be happier if we had a different set of circumstances.

The Truth is, if we are not content within our present circumstances, we are not likely to be happy in any other set of circumstances.

When she was in her fifties, nineteenth-century writer Elizabeth Prentiss learned that her husband would be taking a new job that required them to uproot from their home in New York and move to Chicago. The move meant leaving all their friends and posed a danger to her fragile health. In a letter to a friend, she wrote:

> We want to know no will but God's in this question. . . . The experience of the past winter would impress upon me the fact that place and position have next to nothing to do with happiness; that we can be wretched in a palace, radiant in a dungeon. . . . perhaps this heartbreaking is exactly what we need to remind us . . . that we are pilgrims and strangers on the earth.[4]

George Washington's wife, Martha, expressed the same conviction in a letter written to her friend Mercy Warren:

> I am still determined to be cheerful and happy in whatever situation I may be; for I have also learned from experience that the greater part of our happiness or misery depends on our dispositions and not on our circumstances. We carry the seeds of the one or the other about with us in our minds, wherever we go.[5]

The apostle Paul learned that he could rejoice and be content and fruitful in any circumstance because his joy and well-being were not dependent on his circumstances but on the steadfast love and faithfulness of God and the condition of his relationship with God. That is why he could say,

I have learned to be content whatever the circumstances.
I know what it is to be in need, and I know what it is
to have plenty. I have learned the secret of being content
in any and every situation, whether well fed or hungry,
whether living in plenty or in want.

Philippians 4:11–12

Paul understood that we may not be able to control our circumstances, but our circumstances don't have to control us.

The Truth is that we can trust a wise, loving, sovereign God to control every circumstance of our lives. Joy, peace, and stability come from believing that every circumstance that touches our lives has first been filtered through His fingers of love and is part of a great, eternal plan that He is working out in this world and in our lives.

37. "I SHOULDN'T HAVE TO SUFFER."

Many modern-day evangelistic efforts have promised sinners unending peace, joy, a home in heaven, and a prosperous life between here and there, if they will simply come to Jesus. That kind of preaching, stripped of the call to discipleship and cross bearing, has produced a generation of soft, flabby "disciples" who have no stomach for the battles of the Christian life. When their hopes are dashed by the inevitable trials and tribulations, they whimper and whine and make a dash for the quickest escape route.

By convincing us that our suffering is undeserved or unnecessary, the Enemy succeeds in getting us to resent and resist the will and purposes of God.

The message that was preached by the Lord Jesus Himself and by the apostles who followed Him was a call to take up the cross; it was a call to sign up for battle; it was a call to suffer.

The apostle Paul taught that suffering is an essential course in God's curriculum for all believers: "We must through much tribulation enter into the kingdom of God" (Acts 14:22 KJV).

Arthur Mathews served as a missionary in China from 1938–49, when the Communists took control. He was one of the last China Inland Mission missionaries to leave China in 1953, after being held under house arrest for four years with his wife and daughter. His writings reflect a commitment to self-denial and a willingness to embrace the plan and purposes of God in suffering:

> We tend to look at the circumstances of life in terms of what they may do to our cherished hopes and convenience, and we shape our decisions and reactions accordingly. When a problem threatens, we rush to God, not to seek his perspective, but to ask him to deflect the trouble. Our self-concern takes priority over whatever it is that God might be trying to do through the trouble. . . .
>
> An escapist generation reads security, prosperity, and physical well-being as evidences of God's blessing. Thus when he puts suffering and affliction into our hands, we misread his signals and misinterpret his intentions.[6]

If we do not trust the heart and intentions of God, we will naturally resist suffering. But, as seventeenth-century Puritan author William Law exhorts us, we must learn to welcome and embrace suffering as a pathway to sanctification and a doorway into greater intimacy with God:

> Receive every inward and outward trouble, every disappointment, pain, uneasiness, temptation, darkness, and desolation, with both thy hands, as a true opportunity and blessed occasion of dying to self, and entering into a fuller fellowship with thy self-denying, suffering Saviour.[7]

The Truth is, God is far more interested in our holiness than in our immediate, temporal happiness—He knows that apart from being holy, we can never be truly happy.

The Truth is, it is impossible to be holy apart from suffering. Even Jesus Himself, during His years here on earth, was in some unexplainable way made "perfect through suffering" (Hebrews 2:10); and "although he was a son, he learned obedience from what he suffered" (Hebrews 5:8). We say we want to be like Jesus, and then we resist the very instrument God chooses to fulfill that desire.

All the New Testament authors recognized that there is a redemptive, sanctifying fruit that cannot be produced in our lives apart from suffering. In fact, Peter goes so far as to insist that suffering is our *calling*—not just for some select group of Christian leaders or martyrs but for every child of God: "To this you were called, because Christ suffered for you, leaving you an example, that you should follow in his steps" (1 Peter 2:21).

True joy is not the absence of pain but the sanctifying, sustaining presence of the Lord Jesus *in the midst of* the pain. Through the whole process, whether it be a matter of days, weeks, months, or years, we have His promise:

> The God of all grace, who called you to his eternal glory
> in Christ, after you have suffered a little while, will himself
> restore you and make you strong, firm and steadfast.
>
> *1 Peter 5:10*

🍎 38. "MY CIRCUMSTANCES WILL NEVER CHANGE—THIS WILL GO ON FOREVER."

This lie imprisons many women in hopelessness and despair.

The Truth is, your pain—be it physical affliction, memories of abuse, a troubled marriage, or a heart broken by a wayward child—may go on for a long time. But it will not last forever. It may go on for all of your life down here on this earth. But even a lifetime is not forever.

The Truth is, a moment or two from now (in the light of eternity), when we are in the presence of the Lord, everything that has taken place in this life will be just a breath—a comma.

A woman called a few days ago and asked for counsel in dealing with a complicated and painful situation in her marriage. The situation had been that way for as long as she could remember, and there was no indication of anything changing in the future. In the course of the conversation, I was moved as this dear, suffering wife said, "If it goes on for our whole lives, that's OK. I know that time is short and eternity is long. One day this will all be just a blip on the screen." She spoke not as one who is just resigned to her "fate." She longs for things to be different now. But she has a perspective of time and eternity that is enabling her to be faithful in the midst of the "fire."

Another woman came to me years ago after a conference and said, "I want to thank you for what you said about being faithful to your mate, no matter what." She went on to tell the story of how she had lived for forty years in a marriage to a wicked man. She said, "All through those years, many people—including well-meaning Christians —counseled me to get out of this marriage. But somehow, God kept drawing me back to that vow I had made, and I did not believe it was right to leave." After a pause, she continued, "I'm so glad I waited. You see, a year ago, my husband finally got saved, and God is truly changing him, after all these years. And not only that," she said softly, with tears in her eyes, "you can't believe the incredible changes God has brought about in *my* life as a result of the suffering."

The problem is, we are so earthbound that, to most of us, forty years sounds like *eternity!* We can't fathom enduring that long. If we could only see that forty years—or longer—is inconsequential in the light of eternity.

Regardless of how long our suffering continues, God's Word assures us that it will not last forever.

> Therefore we do not lose heart. . . . For our light and *momentary troubles* are achieving for us an eternal glory that far

outweighs them all. So we fix our eyes not on what is seen,
but on what is unseen. For *what is seen* [i.e., our
current trouble] *is temporary,* but what is unseen
[i.e., the glory that awaits us] is eternal.

2 Corinthians 4:16–18, italics added

I consider that our present sufferings are not worth
comparing with the glory that will be revealed in us.

Romans 8:18

Weeping may endure for a night,
but joy cometh in the morning.

Psalm 30:5 KJV

Your night of weeping may go on for months or even years. But
if you are a child of God, it will not go on forever. God has determined the exact duration of your suffering, and it will not last one
moment longer than He knows is necessary to achieve His holy, eternal purposes in and through your life.

In those cases where there is no relief from pain in this life, we
have literally hundreds of promises in God's Word that one day all suffering will be over, faith will become sight, darkness will be turned
to light, and our faithfulness will be rewarded with unending joy.
He promises that one day,

[the] desert and the parched land will be glad;
the wilderness will rejoice and blossom. . . .
And the ransomed of the LORD . . .
will enter Zion with singing;

everlasting joy will crown their heads.
Gladness and joy will overtake them,
and sorrow and sighing will flee away.

Isaiah 35:1, 10

Regardless of how powerful the forces of darkness seem to be here and now, the final chapter has been written—and God wins! Believing the Truth about what lies ahead will fill us with hope and enable us to persevere between now and then.

39. "I JUST CAN'T TAKE ANY MORE."

Here is another lie the Enemy works hard to get us to believe, because he knows if we do, we will live in defeat and hopelessness. One woman wrote and said:

I have one-year-old twin boys who have been chronically sick with ear infections and colds for two months, causing them to be whiny and irritable constantly. I kept telling myself, my husband, and anyone who would listen, "I can't take it anymore." The lie was a self-fulfilling prophecy, and it was stressing me out. When I finally said, "Yes, I can take it and I will do my duty to them," the greatest part of the tension and stress I was feeling dissolved.

All of us have had seasons when we feel we just can't keep going; we just can't take any more. As with every other area of deception, the key to defeating this lie is to counter it with the Truth. Regardless of what our emotions or our circumstances may tell us, God's Word says, "My grace is sufficient for you" (2 Corinthians 12:9).

Most of us are familiar with that verse. But, when it comes to the circumstances and trials of our lives, few of us really believe it. What we really believe is, "I can't go on . . .

- I can't take one more sleepless night with this sick child;
- I can't continue in this marriage;
- I can't bear to be hurt one more time by my mother-in-law;
- I can't keep making it with three teenagers and a mother with Alzheimer's living in our home. . . ."

However, whether I choose to believe it or not, if I am His child, the Truth is that "His grace *is* sufficient for me." (This is assuming, of course, that I haven't taken on myself responsibilities He never intended me to carry. If the burden is God-given, I can go on by His grace.) His grace is sufficient for every moment, every circumstance, every detail, every need, and every failure of my life.

When I'm exhausted and think I can't possibly face the unfinished tasks that are still before me, *His grace is sufficient for me.*

When I'm having a hard time responding to that family member or that person at the office who really gets under my skin, *His grace is sufficient for me.*

When I am tempted to vent my frustration by speaking harsh words, *His grace is sufficient for me.*

When I've given in to my lust for food for the umpteenth time that day, *His grace is sufficient for me.*

When I blow it with my family and become uptight and even peevish, *His grace is sufficient for me.*

When I don't know which direction to go or what decision to make, *His grace is sufficient for me.*

When my heart is breaking with an overwhelming sense of loss and grief as I stand by the grave of a loved one, *His grace is sufficient for me.*

What do you need God's grace for? Wayward children? Aching body? Unloving husband? No money in the bank? Struggling to raise three kids without a dad in the home? Don't know where next month's rent is coming from? Lost your job? Just moved to a new city and don't know a soul? Church going through a split? Desperately lonely? Weighed down with guilt? Chemically dependent? Hormones going haywire?

Fill in the blank. Whatever your story, whatever your situation, right now, *His grace is sufficient for you*. His divine resources are available to meet your need—no matter how great. That's the Truth. And the Truth will set you free.

Dear child of God, your heavenly Father will never lead you anywhere that His grace will not sustain you. He will never place more upon you than He will give you grace to bear. When the path before you seems hopelessly long, take heart. Lift up your eyes. Look ahead to that day when all suffering will be over. And remember that when you stand before Him, all the tears and sorrows of a lifetime will seem dim in comparison with the beauty and glory of His face. Without a doubt, you will say, "His amazing grace has brought me safely home."

40. "IT'S ALL ABOUT ME."

Lying on my desk are two advertisements—one for a national stationery supplier, the other for a large chain of retail stores. The headline for both ads reads:

It's all about *you*.

The philosophy behind those ad campaigns is almost as old as the human race. In effect, that's exactly what the Serpent said to Eve: "It's all about *you*." It's a campaign he has been running effectively ever since.

One writer observed that "to most people the greatest persons in the universe are themselves. Their lives are made up of endless variations on the word 'me.'"[8]

It's true. In spite of all the talk about poor self-image, our instinctive reaction to life is self-centered: How does this affect *me?* Will this make *me* happy? Why did this have to happen to *me?* What does she think about *me?* It's *my* turn. Where's *my* share? Nobody cares about *my* ideas. He hurt *my* feelings. I've got to have some time for *me.* I need *my* space. He's not sensitive to *my* needs.

It's not enough for us to be the center of our own universe. We want to be the center of everyone else's universe as well—including God's. When others don't bow down before us and devote themselves to promoting our happiness and meeting our needs, we get hurt and start looking for alternate ways to fulfill our egocentric agenda.

You'd think the church would be the one place where things would revolve around God rather than man. But not necessarily so. In his book *Finding God,* Dr. Larry Crabb offers a penetrating analysis of the extent to which the evangelical church has given in to this deception:

> Helping people to feel loved and worthwhile has become the central mission of the church. We are learning not to worship God in self-denial and costly service, but to embrace our inner child, heal our memories, overcome addictions, lift our depressions, improve our self-images, establish self-preserving boundaries, substitute self-love for self-hatred, and replace shame with an affirming acceptance of who we are.
>
> Recovery from pain is absorbing an increasing share of the church's energy. And that is alarming. . . .
>
> We have become committed to relieving the pain behind our problems rather than using our pain to wrestle more passionately with the character and purpose of God. *Feeling better has become more important than finding God.* . . .
>
> As a result, we happily camp on biblical ideas that help us feel loved and accepted, and we pass over Scripture that calls us to higher ground. We twist wonderful truths about God's acceptance, his redeeming love, and our new identity in Christ into a basis for honoring ourselves rather than seeing those truths for what they are: the stunning revelation of a

God gracious enough to love people who hated him, a God worthy to be honored above everyone and everything else.

. . . We have rearranged things so that God is now worthy of honor because he has honored us. "Worthy is the Lamb," we cry, not in response to his amazing grace, but because he has recovered what we value most: the ability to like ourselves. *We now matter more than God.*[9]

The apostle Paul understood that God does not exist for us, but that we exist for Him:

> By him all things were created: things in heaven and on
> earth, visible and invisible, whether thrones or powers or
> rulers or authorities; all things were created by him and for
> him. He is before all things, and in him all things hold
> together. And he is the head of the body, the church; he is
> the beginning and the firstborn from among the dead,
> so that in everything he might have the supremacy.
>
> *Colossians 1:16–18*

Why was Paul able to sing hymns to God in the middle of the night from the belly of a Roman dungeon? How could he stay faithful and "rejoice always," while being stoned, shipwrecked, lied about, and rejected by friends and enemies alike? How could he "rejoice always" when he was hungry and tired? His secret was that he had settled the issue of why he was living. He was not living to please himself or to get his needs fulfilled. From the point of his conversion on the road to Damascus, he had one burning passion: to live for the glory and the pleasure of God. All that mattered to him was knowing Christ and making Him known to others.

> I consider my life worth nothing to me, if only
> I may finish the race and complete the task

the Lord Jesus has given me—the task of
testifying to the gospel of God's grace.

☒

Acts 20:24

The bottom line for Paul was: "To live is Christ." Once that was settled, nothing else mattered much.

CORAM DEO

Coram Deo is a Latin phrase that means "before the face of God." Many years ago, a woman sent me a framed piece on which she had written out in calligraphy a succinct reminder of what it means to function as our Creator designed us to live:

CORAM DEO
Living all of life
in the presence of God
under the authority of God
and to the glory of God.

I want to close this chapter by sharing with you three sketches of women who exemplify what it means to live *coram Deo*.

"Cindy" shared her story with me in a lengthy letter. She got married at the age of eighteen and had three children by the time she was twenty-one. Though she had been baptized as a child, she did not know what it was to have a personal relationship with Jesus Christ. When she was in her thirties, as her mother lay in a hospital in a coma, dying of cancer, Cindy picked up a Gideon Bible and cried out to the Lord to help her. "From that moment on," she wrote, "my heart's desire was to know God."

Over the next several years, her marriage and family life became increasingly rocky. There was a vicious cycle of abusive behavior and language; her fourteen-year-old daughter ran away from home and her two sons were in consistent trouble at school and with the police. At one point, Cindy left her husband for two weeks, intending to divorce him; through a series of circumstances, God gave her a new compassion for him, and she returned home.

In the midst of all the turmoil at home, Cindy attended a meeting at a nearby church, where she heard the Good News of God's love and how Jesus died to save sinners. She gave her heart to Jesus and became a new creature.

Things continued to get worse at home. Her children, now in their teens, were completely out of control. Her daughter ended up on the streets for a year, after her dad would not let her back in the house one day. Subsequently, the daughter married and had five children; she is now going through a divorce, after twenty-five years of marriage. Her father has never been willing to talk to her and does not know his grandchildren or great-grandchildren.

One son was dishonorably discharged from the Marines and spent four years in prison; he and his father are estranged and have not spoken in years.

The other son became a drug addict and was also dishonorably discharged from the military. He was involved in a homicide in a tavern and spent twenty-two years in a penitentiary. Though he made a profession of faith while in prison, he no longer shows any interest in spiritual things.

Cindy concluded her letter by reflecting on the needs in her family and where she fits in to all that is going on:

✿ ✿

There are no Christmases or Thanksgivings here at home. Will my family ever be healed emotionally and spiritually? Only the Lord knows. But God is Lord of my life, and I believe He wants to use me to be a testimony and a light for my family. If I don't show them the truth of God's amazing grace, who will? It would be so easy to just walk away and go to some island where there is peace and joy. But God has chosen me to be where I am, to be a testimony to my unsaved husband and to my children.

How can I help my husband see that one day his pride will be taken away and he will have to face Christ? How can I help my daughter see the truth of God's unconditional love? How can I help my eldest son, who has turned his back on God since leaving prison? How can I help my husband reconcile with his other son and daughter? Only through God's power, wisdom, and love. So with all my heart, mind, body, and soul, I say, "Yes, Lord—whatever You want me to do."

Jennie Thompson is a young woman whose husband went to be with the Lord not long ago, after an intense two-year battle with leukemia. In a letter written three months after Robert's home-going, this widow with four boys ages seven and under expresses an extraordinary perspective on the heart and purposes of God:

The Lord has been faithful in holding us up through this time. I wouldn't in a million years have chosen this path for my life or the lives of my children, but we have learned so much in and through our circumstances that we could never have learned another way. God has been honored and glorified in a way that never could have happened without our circumstances, so I must praise Him for those circumstances.

God is not in the business of making us "happy"; His business is to receive the glory that is due Him as our Creator and almighty God. Our happiness is the by-product of being in and doing His will. That, and only that, is the reason I can be weeping at the graveside of my best friend, my husband, and the father of my children and still be happy.

In the fall of 1998, my dear friend and longtime prayer partner **Janiece Grissom** began to experience numbness and tingling in her hands and then her arms. Early in 1999, after many tests and doctor appointments, a neurologist confirmed that she had Lou Gehrig's disease. Janiece was forty-one years old and the mother of four children, ages four to twelve.

Over the next ten months, the disease took over first one part and then another of her steadily weakening body. Throughout those months, as we had occasion to talk on the phone, Janiece always refused to focus on herself or her prognosis. Invariably, when she would hear my voice, she would say, "Nancy, you've really been on my heart! How can I pray for you?"

In October of that year, I visited with Janiece and her husband in their home in Little Rock. By this time, she was confined to a recliner; she could not use her arms or legs and could speak only with difficulty, as she had lost 50 percent of her lung capacity. Again, I was deeply touched by how God-conscious and God-centered this couple was, even as they faced the ravages of this disease. I remember Janiece saying over and over that evening, "God has been so good to us!" As the evening drew to a close, several of us surrounded her chair, prayed together, and then sang one of her favorite hymns:

> Like a river glorious is God's perfect peace. . . .
> Stayed upon Jehovah, hearts are fully blest—
> Finding as He promised, perfect peace and rest.[10]

Within the next week, Janiece's physical condition began to deteriorate even more rapidly. Because she was unable to swallow, she was taken to the hospital to have a feeding tube inserted. She never returned home. On the evening of December 13, I called her husband to see how she was doing. Her strength was almost gone, and she could not speak above a whisper. "But," Tim said, "the incredible thing is that she is still spending most of her waking hours praying for other people." Within a matter of hours, Janiece breathed her last and was in the presence of the Lord.

Janiece Grissom died the way she had lived—selflessly loving God and others. In her mind, it was never about herself—her health, her comfort, her future. It was all about God—all that mattered was glorifying Him through surrendering to His purposes for her life. Her sole desire, as expressed by the apostle Paul, was that "now as always Christ will be exalted in my body, whether by life or by death" (Philippians 1:20).

Pastor's wife and author Susan Hunt says it beautifully:

> History is the story of redemption. This story is much bigger than I. I am not the main character in the drama of redemption. I am not the point. But by God's grace I am a part of it. My subplot is integral to the whole. It is far more significant to have a small part in this story than to star in my own puny production. This is a cosmic story that will run throughout eternity. Will I play my part with grace and joy, or will I go for the short-run, insignificant story that really has no point?[11]

The Truth is, it's not about you. It's not about me. It's all about Him. The Truth may not change your circumstances—at least not here and now—but it will change *you*. The Truth will set you free.

THE LIE	THE TRUTH
36. IF MY CIRCUMSTANCES WERE DIFFERENT, *I* WOULD BE DIFFERENT.	• My circumstances do not make me what I am; they merely reveal what I am. • If I am not content with my present circumstances, I am not likely to be happy in any other set of circumstances. • I may not be able to control my circumstances, but my circumstances do not have to control me. • Every circumstance that touches my life has first been filtered through His fingers of love.
37. I SHOULDN'T HAVE TO SUFFER.	• It is impossible to be holy apart from suffering. There is a redemptive fruit that cannot be produced in our lives apart from suffering. • We have been called to suffer. • True joy is not the absence of pain, but the presence of the Lord Jesus in the midst of the pain. • Suffering is a pathway to sanctification, a doorway into greater intimacy with God.
38. MY CIRCUMSTANCES WILL NEVER CHANGE—THIS WILL GO ON FOREVER.	• My suffering may last a long time, but it will not last forever. • My painful circumstances will not last one moment longer than God knows is necessary to achieve His eternal purposes in and through my life. • One day, all pain, suffering, and tears will be removed forever.

THE LIE	THE TRUTH
39. I JUST CAN'T TAKE ANY MORE.	• Whatever my circumstance, whatever my situation, His grace is sufficient for me. • God will never place more on me than He will give me grace to bear.
40. IT'S ALL ABOUT ME.	• God is the beginning and ending and center of all things. All things were created by Him and for Him. It's all about Him! • My life is dispensable. I was created for His pleasure and glory.

1. AGREE with God.

What lies have you believed about circumstances and suffering?

_____

_____

2. ACCEPT responsibility.

How has believing those lies manifested itself in the way you live (e.g., attitudes, actions)?

_____

_____

3. AFFIRM the Truth.

Read aloud each of the Truths listed on pages 236–37. Which of these Truths do you particularly need to embrace at this time?

_____

Renew your mind (your thinking) by the Word of God. Read the following passages aloud. What do these verses teach about how to look at difficult or painful circumstances from God's point of view?

Philippians 4:11–13

_____

James 1:2–5

_____

2 Corinthians 4:16–18

_____

2 Corinthians 12:7–10

_____

Hebrews 12:2–11

_____

Revelation 21:4–6

_____

4. ACT on the Truth.

What specific step(s) of action do you need to take to align your life
with the Truth?

_____

_____

5. ASK God to help you walk in the Truth.

*My Great Shepherd, how I thank You that regardless of what happens
to me or around me, You are still God, You are still good, and You are
still on Your throne. Thank You that You use trials and pressures to make
me more dependent on You, to mold me into Your image, to strengthen
my faith, and to glorify Yourself in the world. Please forgive me for all
the times I have resented, resisted, or run from painful circumstances,
rather than choosing to embrace the cross. Thank You that You will never
leave me or forsake me and that nothing can come into my life that has
not first been filtered through Your fingers of love. Help me to trust You
when I cannot see the outcome. Set me free from preoccupation with myself and with how my circumstances affect me. May my responses to
problems and pressure reveal to the world the greatness and sufficiency of
Your grace. Thank You for Your promise that one day all sorrow and suffering will be over. May I be faithful in loving, trusting, and glorifying
You until that day. In Jesus' name. Amen.*

WALKING IN THE TRUTH

CHAPTER TEN

COUNTERING LIES WITH THE TRUTH

We have examined many different lies that are widely believed by Christian women today. However, we have by no means exhausted the lies in the Enemy's arsenal. Deception has endless variations, which Satan tailors to our natural bents. Like a seasoned fisherman, he selects the lure that he knows is most likely to attract his intended prey—the one we are least likely to consider harmful. He does not care what we believe, as long as we don't believe the Truth. The Truth is the only thing he cannot withstand; it causes his kingdom and his control to crumble.

Before we take a final, close-up look at the Truth that counters Satan's lies (chapter 11), let's step back and review the two major points of this book:

BELIEVING LIES PLACES US IN BONDAGE.

THE TRUTH HAS THE POWER TO SET US FREE.

We have seen that the progression toward bondage begins when we *listen* to Satan's lies. We may think it won't hurt to be exposed to ungodly ways of thinking in the television programs and movies we watch, the music we listen to, the books and magazines we read, and the friends we associate with. But we do not realize how subtly those deceptive philosophies can influence our thinking. That is why God promises a special blessing to those who do not "walk in the counsel of the wicked or stand in the way of sinners or sit in the seat of mockers" (Psalm 1:1).

Once we permit Satan's lies to gain an entrance into our minds, the progression continues as we *dwell* on those lies. If we do not immediately reject deceptive ways of thinking, but allow ourselves to entertain them in our minds, sooner or later we will begin to *believe* them. And what we believe inevitably is what we will *act* on.

When we *act* on the lies we have believed, we begin to establish patterns in our lives that ultimately lead to bondage.

"Shondra's" testimony illustrates how believing things that aren't true leads to bondage in our relationship with God and others.

Believing that God didn't really love and accept me, and that I was worthless, put me in bondage to perfectionism and seeking performance-based approval. In my relationship with God, I felt as though I could only please Him by being a perfect Christian. I believed that if I sinned, He would not accept me. I was defeated in my Christian walk because I knew I was not without sin; my faulty thinking condemned me and put me in bondage.

My pride became evident in two ways: (1) I denied my sin— I couldn't bear to admit I had failed to be perfect, because I did not want God to find me unacceptable. (2) I relied on my own self-fueled attempts to be holy, even though my human effort always resulted in failure—which made me feel even more unacceptable to God. This cycle of effort/failure/sin/guilt kept me from truly experiencing forgiveness, freedom, and joy in my relationship with God.

In my relationships with others, I sought to find approval and acceptance in making them happy. I became a people-pleaser and a "yes-woman." I rarely considered what God wanted me to do concerning interpersonal relationships, because keeping people happy was critical to my feeling worthwhile. My relationships were marked by dishonesty, as I was driven to avoid confrontation or causing disappointment. I wore a mask to cover my real feelings, so I would not bother anyone with my problems. I felt very alone because no one really knew me, and I became bitter and frustrated toward the people who "used" me (even though I practically sent them an invitation to do so).

I could not accept any personal limitations. I viewed any mistake or shortcoming as utter failure and proof of my worthlessness. I consistently set goals too high to reach and inevitably fell short. I demanded absolute perfection of myself, and criticized myself mercilessly when I couldn't achieve it. I was miserable. The self-imposed pressure I lived under became unbearable and sent me into depression in my midthirties.

A few months ago, I realized I was in bondage and needed to be set free from the tyranny of the lies I was believing. However, I was still hesitant to cry out to the Lord for help, because deep inside, I felt that He would reject me if I admitted my weak and sinful condition.

When Shondra attended a conference where she learned about the danger of deception and the power of the Truth, it was like a light went on in her heart; for the first time she began to have hope:

During the conference, the Holy Spirit deeply convicted me about my neglect of God's Word. His Word is Truth, and if I am to defeat the stronghold of Satan's lies in my life, I need to saturate my life with God's Word. I really believe that this is my only hope. I cannot make it without consistent time exposing my mind and heart to the Truth of God's Word. I have committed to spending time every day reading and meditating on God's Truth. I realize that renewing my mind will be a process of continually confronting the lies and refuting them with God's Word. I know that the Scripture has supernatural power, and I claim His promise that the Truth will set me free!

As you have read this book, have you recognized any specific area(s) where you have listened to, believed, and acted on lies? If so, there are likely one or more areas of bondage in your life—areas where you are not walking in freedom before God. These may be major, deeply rooted issues, or they may be matters that seem relatively insignificant. They may be areas where you have been defeated and cried out for deliverance for years. Or they may be issues you are just now recognizing for the first time.

Regardless, as we have seen, the pathway from bondage to freedom involves at least three steps:

1. Identify the area(s) of bondage or sinful behavior.
2. Identify the lie(s) at the root of that bondage or behavior.
3. Replace the lie(s) with the Truth.

The Truth has the power to overcome every lie. That is what the Enemy doesn't want you to realize. As long as you believe his lies, he can keep you in bondage. But once you know the Truth and start believing and acting on it, the prison doors will swing open and you will be set free.

The Truth has the power to set us free (John 8:32) and to protect our minds and hearts from deceptive thoughts and feelings. There are moments when I feel besieged with emotions or thoughts I know are not of God—angry, irrational, fearful, controlling, or resentful thoughts. That is when I need to run to the Truth for refuge. God's Word promises: "He shall cover thee with his feathers, and under his wings shalt thou trust: *his truth* shall be thy shield and buckler" (Psalm 91:4 KJV, italics added).

The Truth has the power to sanctify us—to purify our minds, our hearts, and our spirits. Just before He went to the cross, Jesus reminded His disciples about the cleansing power of His Word (John 15:3). Two chapters later, He prayed, "Father, . . . sanctify them by the truth; your word is truth" (John 17:17). Often, as I approach the Scripture, I pray, "Father, please wash me with Your Word. Your Word is Truth. Use the Truth to cleanse my heart, purify my mind, bathe me in Your Word."

CHOOSING THE PATHWAY OF TRUTH

Each time the Enemy bombards us with lies, we must learn to counsel our hearts according to the Truth and to act on the Truth, regardless of what our human reason or our feelings tell us.

When I find myself giving in to weariness, frustration, or my flesh; when my mind and emotions are swirling with things I know aren't true, I try to stop and identify the Truth that counters those lies.

I speak the Truth to myself—sometimes aloud, and, if necessary, over and over again—until the Truth displaces and replaces the lies I have been believing. I cry out to God for grace to act on what I know to be true. Time after time, I have been amazed at the power of the Truth to calm my turbulent emotions and to restore settledness and sanity to my confused thoughts.

Some time ago, I was in a meeting where some long-simmering issues came to a full boil. In the course of the discussion, one individual made some statements about me that, from my perspective, were unfounded and extremely damaging. I was devastated.

When I got home that evening, I cried and cried. Over the next several hours, the Enemy began to wreak havoc with my mind and my emotions. All I could think about was how wrong the other person had been, and how deeply I had been wounded. I began to let resentful, vindictive thoughts take root in my mind. I resurrected other, past offenses that I thought were long gone, and became obsessed with trying to figure out how to vindicate myself and prove my innocence. My emotions spun out of control and I careened into a downward spiral of anger and self-pity.

Looking back now, I realize I was listening to and believing a number of lies . . . lies like:

- "So-and-so" was being malicious and intended to hurt me.
- I deserve to be treated better; I shouldn't have to go through this.
- The other person was 100 percent at fault. I was totally innocent.
- I cannot forgive "so-and-so."
- The damage cannot be undone.
- Our relationship can never be restored.
- "So-and-so" *made* me angry.
- I have a right to be angry.
- I have a right to defend myself and to be sure others know the truth.
- I just can't let this go. I can't help the way I feel.

Believing those lies resulted in hours of inner turmoil and struggle.

The next morning, as I opened my Bible and began to read where I had left off the day before, I found myself in Matthew, chapters 5 and 6. There I had a head-on collision with the Truth:

Blessed are the meek. . . .
Blessed are the merciful, for they will be shown mercy. . . .
Blessed are the peacemakers. . . .

I tell you, Do not resist an evil person. If someone strikes you
on the right cheek, turn to him the other also. . . . Love your
enemies and pray for those who persecute you. . . .

If you forgive men when they sin against you, your heavenly
Father will also forgive you. But if you do not forgive men
their sins, your Father will not forgive your sins.

Matthew 5:5, 7, 9, 39, 44; 6:14–15

Now I had a choice. Would I continue to believe the lies, or would I embrace the Truth? That's when the battle really started. My emotions wanted to hold on to the offense. I wanted to nurse the grudge; I wanted to stay angry; I wanted somehow to hurt the person who had hurt me. But in my heart I knew that choice would lead to bondage.

As I knelt before the Lord, with the open Bible in front of me, I grappled with the Truth. I knew I had to forgive—that I must release the offender and the offense. I *felt* there was no way I could forgive; but deep down, I knew the issue wasn't that I *couldn't* forgive—it was that I didn't *want* to forgive. I knew if I was going to walk in the Truth, I had to relinquish any right to get even or to withhold love from that individual.

I began to speak the Truth to myself—to counsel my heart according to the Truth. I reminded myself of the consequences of refusing to forgive, of the mercy I would forfeit if I refused to extend mercy to others, and of the blessings I would receive if I was willing to obey His commands.

I knew I could not wait until I *felt* like forgiving—that I had to *choose* to obey God, and that my emotions would follow sooner or later. There on my knees, with my emotions still battling, I finally waved the white flag of surrender. In essence, I said to the Lord, "You win." I yielded myself and the entire matter to the Lord and agreed, as an act of my will, to forgive the one who had hurt me. Hard as it was, I agreed to "let it go."

The emotional release did not come immediately. For some time, I found myself still feeling "bruised"; at times, I was tempted to resume my emotional temper tantrum or to subtly retaliate. But, by God's grace, I continued to speak the Truth to my heart and to make the choice to act on the Truth. Out of obedience to God's Word, I began to look for ways to rebuild the relationship and invest in the life of the one who had hurt me.

In the weeks that followed, my emotions gradually followed my will. The Truth had countered the lies; my spirit was free. In time, God gave me further insight into the original situation; He shed light on why I had reacted the way I had and showed me some deeper heart issues that I had not realized needed to be addressed. I am grateful that He loved me enough to orchestrate circumstances to bring those issues to the surface, and I thank Him for using that experience to make me more like Jesus.

THE TRANSFORMING POWER OF TRUTH

Freedom from bondage is the sweet fruit of knowing, believing, and acting on the Truth. And how can we know the Truth? We must remember that the Truth is not merely an idea or a philosophy. The Truth is a Person—the Lord Jesus Christ. He said of Himself, "*I am* the way and *the truth* and the life" (John 14:6, italics added). Jesus did not point men to a religious system; He pointed them to Himself. To those who claimed to be His followers, He said,

> If you hold to my teaching, you are really my disciples.
> Then you will know the truth, and the truth will set you
> free. . . . If the Son sets you free, you will be free indeed.
>
> *John 8:31–32, 36*

True freedom is found in a vital, growing relationship with the Lord Jesus. Jesus (the living Word of God) has revealed Himself in the Scripture (the written Word of God). If we want to know Him, if we want to know the Truth, we must devote ourselves to the reading, study, and meditation of His Word. There is no substitute and there are no shortcuts. The Enemy is constantly confronting us with his lies. In order to combat his deception, our minds and hearts must be filled with the Lord Jesus and saturated with His Word.

But it is not enough to know the Truth. We must also *surrender* to the Truth. That means we must be willing to change our thinking or our lifestyle in any areas where they do not square with the Word of God. Millions of professing Christians are deceived; they are walking in ways that simply are not biblical. Their values, their responses, their relationships, their choices, and their priorities reveal that they have bought into the lie of the Enemy and embraced the world's way of thinking.

We cannot assume a particular viewpoint is true just because everyone else thinks that way—or because it is what we have always believed, or because a well-known Christian author promotes that position, or because a well-meaning friend or counselor says it is right. Everything we believe and everything we do must be evaluated in the light of God's Word. That is our only absolute authority.

Living according to Truth requires a conscious choice to reject deception and to embrace the Truth. That is why the psalmist prayed, "Keep me from deceitful ways. . . . I have chosen the way of truth" (Psalm 119:29–30).

Every time we open the Scripture or hear the Word proclaimed, it ought to be with the prayer that God will open our eyes to see any areas where we have been deceived, and with a heart attitude that says, "Lord, Your Word is Truth; I will submit to whatever You say. Whether I like it or not, whether I feel like it or not, whether I agree with it or not, whether it makes sense or not, I choose to place my life under the authority of Your Word—I will obey."

Once we know the Truth and are walking according to the Truth that we know, God wants to make us instruments to draw others to the Truth.

Then we will no longer be infants, tossed back and forth
by the waves, and blown here and there by every wind
of teaching and by the cunning and craftiness of men
in their deceitful scheming. Instead, *speaking the truth*
in love, we will in all things grow up into him who is
the Head, that is, Christ. . . . Therefore each of you
must put off falsehood and speak *truthfully* to
his neighbor, for we are all members of one body.

Ephesians 4:14–15, 25, italics added

As I shared in the introduction, the burden that gave birth to this book was the longing to see women set free through the Truth. That vision is expressed in the last verses of the book of James:

> If one of you should wander from the truth and someone should bring him back, remember this: Whoever turns a sinner from the error of his way will save him from death and cover over a multitude of sins.
>
> *James 5:19–20*

The idea of "turning sinners from the error of their way" is largely foreign in our day. The hue and cry of our postmodern culture is "tolerance," which means: "You can live however you want to live, but don't try to tell me what's right for me—it's none of your business how I choose to live my life." As deception has inundated our culture, many believers have become hesitant to stand for the Truth, for fear of being labeled as intolerant or narrow-minded.

Many Christians manifest this "live and let live" attitude, not only toward the world, but also in relation to other believers who are not walking in the Truth. They don't want to "rock the boat" or to be considered judgmental. It seems easier just to let things go.

We must remember that in Christ and in His Word, we have the Truth that sets people free. That is Good News! And it is essential news. There is no other way for those we know and love to be delivered from darkness, deception, and death. If we truly care about them, we will prayerfully and actively seek to restore them to God's way of thinking.

We must learn the Truth, believe it, surrender to it, and live it out—even when it flies in the face of our culture. Then we must proclaim the Truth with boldness, conviction, and compassion, seeking to turn sinners from the error of their way and to restore those who have wandered from the Truth.

CHAPTER ELEVEN

THE TRUTH
THAT SETS
US FREE

I n the midst of writing this book, there have been times when I have found myself believing and acting on some of the very lies I was addressing: "I don't have time to do everything I'm supposed to do!" "I can afford to shortcut my time with the Lord this morning." "I can't control my emotions." "I'm acting this way because I'm so tired . . . because I've had so many interruptions . . . because I've got so much to do . . ." "I can't take any more!"

Again and again, in hectic, hassled, or hurting moments, God has directed my heart back to the Truth. As I listen to the Truth, meditate on it, believe it, and surrender to it, the Spirit of God sets me free—my mind and emotions are stabilized and I am able to look at my circumstances from God's perspective. The longer I walk with God, the more I am in awe of the power of the Truth!

We have already looked at many of Satan's lies and the corresponding Truth that counters each lie. In this final chapter, I want to highlight twenty-two of those Truths that I believe are particularly crucial for women in our day to believe and embrace. These are key Truths I find myself going back to over and over again. They form a solid foundation and a protective fortress for my mind, will, and emotions. This is the Truth that sets me free; it is the Truth that will set you free.

Rather than skimming through this chapter, let me encourage you to take time to savor these liberating, life-changing Truths. Say each Truth aloud—again and again and again—until your thinking becomes aligned with God's way of thinking. You may even want to memorize this list, along with the key Scriptures that correspond to each Truth.

In the days ahead, anytime you realize you are believing lies, go back and review this list; renew your mind; counsel your heart according to the Truth.

1. *God is good* (Psalms 119:68; 136:1). When the sun is shining and you have money in the bank and you're healthy and everyone thinks you're wonderful, it's not hard to believe that God is good. But when you lose your job or a loved one is diagnosed with a terminal illness or your church goes through a nasty split or your husband says he doesn't want to be married to you anymore, the Enemy will move in and cause you to question God's goodness.

The Truth is, regardless of the circumstances, regardless of what we feel, regardless of what we think, God *is* good, and everything He does is good.

2. *God loves me and wants me to have His best* (Romans 8:32, 38–39). God doesn't love us because we're lovable or worthy, but because He is love. There is absolutely nothing we can do to earn or deserve His love. We cannot comprehend such unconditional love; but if we believe it and receive it, His love will transform our lives.

Because God is good and loves us perfectly, we can be confident that He longs for us to experience all the joy in life He designed us to know. He knows we will only find this true and lasting joy and fulfillment in Him. He loves us so much, He insists we come to Him, where alone we can be fully satisfied.

3. *I am complete and accepted in Christ* (Ephesians 1:4–6). You may have been rejected by a parent, a mate, a friend, or a child. But if you

are in Christ, you are accepted in Him. We don't have to perform to be made acceptable to Him. We don't have to jump through all kinds of spiritual "hoops." In fact, there is not one thing we can do to make ourselves acceptable to a holy God. Yet we—fallen, condemned, unworthy sinners—can stand before God clean and unashamed, acceptable in His sight. How? Because Jesus—the pure, sinless Son of God—is acceptable to Him, and we stand in Him.

4. *God is enough* (Psalm 23:1). "The LORD is my shepherd; I shall not want" (KJV). You have probably known that verse since you were a small child. But do you believe it? Do you really believe that He is *your* Shepherd? The Truth is, if we have Him, we have everything we need for our present peace and happiness.

5. *God can be trusted* (Isaiah 28:16). God keeps His promises. He has promised never to leave or forsake us (Hebrews 13:5). He has promised that those who trust in Him will never be disappointed. From time to time, I have to remind myself: "God has never once let me down—and He's not going to start now!" After years of struggling and striving, this Truth is where "Colleen" finally found a resting place for her heart:

✳ ✳

I fully believe, for the first time, that God can be completely trusted. I am free from the need to figure out this world and my place in it. I can rest in the One who owns the world and trust Him to guide, instruct, protect, comfort, and bring me joy.

✳ ✳

6. *God doesn't make any mistakes* (Isaiah 46:10). Other people may make serious mistakes that affect our lives. But God is always fulfilling His eternal purposes, and they cannot be thwarted by any human failure. If we are in Christ, our lives are in His hand, and nothing can touch our lives that has not first been "filtered through His fingers of love."

Even when Job was suffering unspeakably and all those devilish darts were being thrown at him, God was still in control. Satan had to get permission from God to touch His servant. God determines the intensity and the duration of the pain. He makes no mistakes with His children's lives. Someone has said, "God's will is exactly what we would choose, if we knew what God knows." When we stand in eternity looking back on this earthly existence, we will know by sight what we can only see now by faith: He has done all things well.

7. *God's grace is sufficient for me* (2 Corinthians 12:9). As a child of God, I will never face a circumstance that exceeds His grace. Where sin abounds, grace does much more abound. When I am weak, He is strong. When I am empty, He is full. When I have no resources of my own left, His resources have not begun to be depleted.

The Truth is, whatever you are going through right now, His grace is sufficient for you. Whatever you will go through tomorrow—or next year or fifty years from now—His grace will be sufficient for you then.

His grace is sufficient to deal with the memories, wounds, and failures of the most scarred or sordid past. His grace is sufficient for a lifetime of singleness or for a half century of marriage to an ungodly man. His grace is sufficient for the single mother trying to raise four children. His grace is sufficient for the mother of three toddlers—or three teenagers. His grace is sufficient for the woman caring for her elderly parents, for the empty nester, for the woman going through the change of life, for the widow living on Social Security, and for the invalid in a nursing home.

We need to speak the Truth to ourselves; we need to speak it to each other. In every season, in every circumstance, His grace *is* sufficient. It is sufficient for me; it is sufficient for you.

8. *The blood of Christ is sufficient to cover all my sin* (1 John 1:7). There is not a sin I have ever committed or a sin I could ever commit that cannot be forgiven and covered by the all-sufficient sacrifice of Jesus' blood. This should not cause us to take sin more lightly; to the contrary, the realization that our sin required the lifeblood of the Lord

Jesus should leave us broken and humble in spirit, and determined to choose the pathway of obedience, by the power of His indwelling Holy Spirit.

The psalmist understood both the enormity of his sin and the even greater enormity of God's mercy toward repentant sinners: "If thou, LORD, shouldest mark iniquities, O Lord, who shall stand? But there is forgiveness with thee, that thou mayest be feared" (Psalm 130:3–4 KJV).

9. *The Cross of Christ is sufficient to conquer my sinful flesh* (Romans 6:6–7). Through the death of Christ and my union with Him, I have been set free from the dominion and power of sin. I am no longer a slave to sin. When I do sin, it is not because I couldn't help myself; it is because I chose to yield to my old master. The Truth is, I don't have to sin (Romans 6:14).

10. *My past does not have to plague me* (1 Corinthians 6:9–11). I love that passage where Paul makes this point to a group of believers, some of whom have had quite a checkered past. He reminds them that sin does separate from God; then he assures them that through Christ, the worst of sinners can be made clean and new.

Do you not know that the wicked will not inherit the kingdom of God? Do not be deceived: Neither the sexually immoral nor idolaters nor adulterers nor male prostitutes nor homosexual offenders nor thieves nor the greedy nor drunkards nor slanderers nor swindlers will inherit the kingdom of God. *And that is what some of you were. But you were washed,* you were sanctified, you were justified in the name of the Lord Jesus Christ and by the Spirit of our God.

1 Corinthians 6:9–11, italics added

You may have been an adulterer, a murderer, an alcoholic, or a lesbian; you may have aborted a child or been sexually promiscuous; you may have been a slave to lust or anger or food or pride. But if you are in Christ, you are no longer what you once were. You are not the same person. You have been cleansed by the blood of Jesus, set apart for His holy purposes, and declared righteous in the eyes of God.

After attending a conference where this Truth was taught, "Lisa" wrote to share with me how the Truth was setting her free from the torment of her past failure:

What can I possibly say about the selfishness of my abortion? How do you forgive yourself for murder? It can't be undone. God could have punished me by making me barren—He didn't. He could have made my kids unhealthy or challenged—He didn't. For twenty-seven years, I have felt that without punishment, I couldn't pay the debt I felt I owed. This weekend I have released my life to God and am receiving His forgiveness. Instead of shame, I have godly sorrow. All those years ago, I put a tight seal on my heart. I swore I would never allow myself to love again. Now God is prying off that seal. I am free to love again and to let others love me. The stronghold is gone.

The Truth is that our past—our upbringing, the ways we have been wronged, and the ways we have wronged others—these things do not have to be hindrances. In fact, by God's grace, they can actually become stepping-stones to greater victory and fruitfulness.

11. *God's Word is sufficient to lead me, teach me, and heal me* (Psalms 19:7; 107:20; 119:105). Many believers in our generation have lost confidence in the power of the Word of God to radically and lastingly change lives, to deliver people from bondage, and to reveal the will of God for our lives. The Scripture is viewed as one of a number of

valuable resources, or as a last resort, after everything else has been tried.

The Truth is, the Word of God is alive and powerful; it is medicine for troubled hearts and peace for plagued minds. It is a lamp for our feet and a light for our path. Whatever our need, whatever our circumstances, the Word of God is sufficient to meet that need. And it is sufficient to meet the needs of those we love.

People around us who are hurting and needy don't need to hear our opinions and suggestions. They need to know what God says. They need to know His commands, His promises, and His ways. If we really want to help people, we must point them to the Truth and prayerfully and lovingly show them how to apply the Truth to their situation.

12. *Through the power of His Holy Spirit, God will enable me to do anything He commands me to do* (1 Thessalonians 5:24; Philippians 2:13). God does not command us to do anything that He does not give us the grace to obey, as we depend on Him. That means, for example, that

- there is *no one* we cannot forgive (Mark 11:25);
- there is *no one* we cannot love (Matthew 5:44);
- we *can* give thanks in all things (1 Thessalonians 5:18);
- we *can* be content in every circumstance (Hebrews 13:5).

The issue is not that we *can't* obey God—that we *can't* forgive that parent who hurt us so deeply, that we *can't* love that colleague at work, that we *can't* give thanks in the midst of the storm, or that we *can't* be content with our one-bedroom apartment.

The real issue is that we *won't* forgive, we are *unwilling* to love, and we *refuse* to give thanks and to be content with what God has provided. Obedience is a choice made in dependence on the supernatural power of God. By the enabling power of the Holy Spirit, we can *choose* to forgive, *choose* to let Him love others through us, *choose* to give thanks in every circumstance, and *choose* to be content.

13. *I am responsible before God for my behavior, responses, and choices* (Ezekiel 18:19–22). One of the most liberating truths I learned as a young teenager was that God does not hold me accountable for the actions of others but that I am responsible for how I respond to them, regardless of how they treat me.

We may not be able to control the circumstances that come into our lives—we had no choice about the home we were born into, our overall physical appearance, our upbringing, and many other factors that have influenced and shaped our lives. But, by God's grace, we do not have to be victims; we can control how we respond to the circumstances He has allowed to come into our lives.

When we stop blaming other people and circumstances for sinful behaviors or negative patterns in our lives, when we begin to assume personal responsibility for our own choices, we will be released from the sense that we are helpless victims. We will be free to obey God, regardless of our circumstances.

14. *I will reap whatever I sow* (Galatians 6:7–8). The older I get, the more conscious I am of the law of the harvest in my life. Virtually all the patterns in my life today are the fruit—for better or worse—of choices I made years ago. As a young girl, I had no idea how important those seemingly insignificant choices would become—the books I read, the people I spent time with, the way I responded to authority, the way I spent my free time, my study habits; today I am living with the harvest of those and countless other choices.

In the same way, the choices we make today will have consequences down the road, not only in our own lives, but in the lives of others for generations to come. Every selfish, sinful, or indulgent choice I make today is sowing a seed that will reap a multiplied harvest. And every act of obedience is a seed that will produce a multiplied harvest of blessing in my life and in the lives of those I love. The harvest is rarely immediate. But it will come.

15. *The pathway to true joy is to relinquish control* (Matthew 16:25; Luke 1:38; 1 Peter 5:7). As we have seen, one of the consequences

of the Fall is that we as women have a drive to be in control. In a thousand subtle—and not-so-subtle—ways, we attempt to exert control over others and over our environment. The fact is, no matter how hard we try, we are not in control. Yet we strive, manipulate, worry, and dominate—all in a vain attempt to control that which we can't control anyway.

The only way to experience true freedom and peace is to let go of the reins—to relinquish all control to God, believing that He can be trusted to manage all that concerns us. Last week, I found myself battling resentment toward a colleague who had disappointed me. As we women are prone to do, I mulled the situation over in my mind—again and again and again. Realizing that this was really a battle for control, I called a dear friend and asked her to pray for me. As we prepared to hang up, she said, "Nancy, I don't quite know how to say this, but remember . . . *you're not God.*" Ouch.

Why is it so hard to let God be God? Why is it so hard to turn over to Him the management of the universe? The Truth is, He *is* in control. He loves us, and He isn't going to fall asleep on the job or let something slip by His notice. When we refuse to let go of the reins, we are really vying for His job. The pathway to freedom is to relinquish all control of our own lives, of our families, and of every circumstance in our lives. Not until then will we see Him do what only He can do.

16. *The greatest freedom I can experience is found through submission to God-ordained authority* (Ephesians 5:21). When we resist authority, we become more vulnerable to Satan's attacks and to sin, even as Eve sinned when she acted apart from the authority of her husband. On the other hand, when we willingly take our place under God-ordained authority, we are granted God's protective covering, we release Him to work in the lives of those in authority over us, we reveal to the world the beauty of God's created order, we proclaim His right to rule over the universe, Satan is defeated in his attempts to dethrone God, and we cooperate with God in establishing His kingdom.

17. *In the will of God, there is no higher, holier calling than to be a wife and mother* (Titus 2:4–5). True fulfillment and joy are found through discovering why God made us and then embracing that created purpose and design. God designed the woman to be a helper to her husband and a bearer and nurturer of life. Marriage and motherhood are God's norm for most women.

God's calling for the married woman centers on her roles in the home. Paul urged Titus to be sure that the younger women in his church were taught

> to love their husbands and children, to be self-controlled and pure, to be busy at home, to be kind, and to be subject to their husbands, so that no one will malign the word of God.

Titus 2:4–5

For a wife and mother, no career, no hobby, no relationship, no priority is more important. A job outside the home may offer greater affirmation and produce more visible and immediate results. It may provide material conveniences that would not otherwise be possible. But to make a home, to be united with a man in glorifying God on this earth, to nurture and tend the lives of children and grandchildren, to train and mold the next generation, to deny oneself and lay down one's life on behalf of others—there is no higher calling and no greater joy.

18. *Personal holiness is more important than temporal happiness* (Ephesians 5:26–27). Contrary to the world's way of thinking, happiness here and now is not the highest good; nor is it a right.

God did not save us to make us happy in a temporal sense—He saved us to "redeem us from all wickedness and to purify for himself a people that are his very own, eager to do what is good" (Titus 2:14). The Lord Jesus left His home in heaven, came down to this earth, and gave His life, not so we could live for ourselves and our own pleasure, but so we could be free to live for the One for whose pleasure we were created.

To choose the pathway of holiness will sometimes require sacrificing our personal comfort and convenience. But any sacrifice we make is temporary, and cannot be compared with the joy and fulfillment we will gain in eternity. Only through seeking to be holy can we ever experience true happiness.

19. *God is more concerned about changing me and glorifying Himself than about solving my problems* (Romans 8:29). When we experience problems, our natural instinct is to demand solutions. If we do not recognize and embrace God's purposes and process in our lives, we will become obsessed with finding a way out of our problems. We will become despondent and angry when God does not "cooperate" with our agenda.

The Truth is, God does not exist to solve our problems. It's not that He doesn't care about the things that matter to us; He does. But everything that matters to us must be subordinate to what matters most to Him.

What matters most to Him is that every created being reflect His glory. His agenda is to do whatever is necessary to conform us to His image. Some of the problems that cause us to chafe the most are actually instruments He has designed to fulfill His ultimate purpose in our lives. To demand a solution or an escape from that impossible boss, that financial situation, that health problem, or that messy marriage may cause us to forfeit a far higher good that He is seeking to bring about in our lives. How foolish and shortsighted it is to reject or resist problems that may be the very means He has designed to mold us into the image of His Son.

20. *It is impossible to be godly without suffering* (1 Peter 5:10). Suffering takes on a whole different perspective when we realize that it is an essential tool in the hand of God to conform us to the image of Jesus. The process of sanctification takes place as we embrace our suffering, rather than running from it or resenting it.

In the book of Jeremiah, we find a vivid picture of what happens if we do not allow suffering to do its purifying work in our lives:

Moab has been at rest from youth,
like wine left on its dregs,
not poured from one jar to another—
she has not gone into exile.
So she tastes as she did,
and her aroma is unchanged.

Jeremiah 48:11

In the process of making wine in Jeremiah's day, the juice from the grapes was poured into a wineskin and left to sit for several weeks, until the bitter dregs or sediment settled onto the bottom. Then it was poured into another wineskin so more dregs could be separated. This process was repeated again and again, until all the dregs had been removed and the wine was pure and sweet.

The nation of Moab had a history of relative ease and comfort; she had not been through the purifying process of being "poured" from suffering to suffering. As a result, the thick, bitter dregs of her sin remained in her—she was "unchanged." Suffering is God's means of pouring us from one jar to another—of unsettling us—so the dregs of self and sin can be separated out, until the pure, sweet wine of His Spirit is all that remains.

21. *My suffering will not last forever* (2 Corinthians 4:17–18). When it seems that we are constantly in the fire, repeatedly being "poured" from one jar to another, our emotions tell us this will go on forever. That is when we need to remind ourselves of the Truth: There will be an end to the process. It will not go on forever.

All suffering is purposeful and intentional. God has a specific objective in mind for our suffering. He knows exactly the intensity and the duration that are needed to fulfill His purposes. He will not allow our suffering to last any longer or to be any more severe than is necessary to accomplish His will.

God has promised that one day "there will be no more death or mourning or crying or pain . . ." (Revelation 21:4). So, dear child of God, when your eyes are filled with tears and there seems to be no hope, take courage. Lift up your head, give thanks, endure, and know that it will not be long before your faith will be rewarded with the sight of the One who has promised to be with you to the end.

22. *It's not about me; it's all about Him* (Colossians 1:16–18; Revelation 4:11)! I need frequent reminders that this world was not created to revolve around me. The entire universe—including you and me—was created to revolve around the One who is high and lifted up and seated on His throne.

God's eternal purposes and plans are far more important than the things that fill our vision and consume our thinking. My bank balance, my aches and pains, my hurt feelings, my needs and wants—these all pale into insignificance when I remember that "It's not about me; it's all about Him."

Before we can respond in a godly way to the circumstances of life, we must first settle this basic issue: What is my purpose in life? If our goal in life is to be happy or accepted or loved, then anything that threatens our well-being will be an enemy—an obstacle to fulfilling our objective.

On the other hand, once we agree with God that we exist for His pleasure and His glory, we can accept whatever comes into our lives as part of His sovereign will and purpose. We will not resent, resist, or reject the "hard things," but embrace them as friends, sovereignly designed by God to make us like Jesus and to bring glory to Himself. We will be able to look into His face and say, "It's not about me. It's about You. If it pleases You, it pleases me. All that matters is that You are glorified."

❧ EPILOGUE ❧

Dear diary,

*One of our great-grandsons, Kenan, stopped by today with his
wife and two of their daughters to bring us some fresh fruits and
vegetables from their garden. Our family has been so good to us,
especially now that we are older and experiencing more physical
limitations.*

*My eyesight continues to deteriorate. Yet, in many ways, I be-
lieve I am just now beginning to really see. The fact is, years ago,
when my eyes were young and strong, I was so very blind. I didn't
see how foolish I was to believe the Serpent. I didn't see the heartache that one wrong choice would bring into our lives. I didn't see
the pain our children would reap. Although I know God holds
Adam ultimately responsible for our first sin and the curse that
resulted, I still feel the weight of yielding to the Serpent's lies.*

*All I could see at the time was something I wanted very badly
—something I thought I needed. I got what I wanted, but I never
could have imagined all that would come with it. That moment of
indulgence brought such pain and regret.*

*Only now, after years of running and hiding and hurting, can
I see how much God loves us and how He has always had our*

best interests at heart. I see clearly now how right His ways are and why it is so important to listen to Him and to do things His way. I only wish I had not wasted so many years believing things that weren't true.

When I think back, it is amazing how merciful God has been to us. After that awful day, He could have written us off forever. But He has never stopped pursuing a relationship with us. After we lost our two sons, God gave us Seth—and then four more sons and daughters. Seth, in particular, represents the restoration and joy God has brought to our lives.

God also promised that one day, there will be another Son. The Serpent will attack and wound Him, as he did us. Then the Son will strike back and deal a final, fatal blow to the Serpent.

It was I, as a woman, along with my husband, who brought this fallen condition on us all those years ago. I can never undo the damage I have done. But—what grace!—God has said that He will use a woman to bring this Son into the world. Through Him, all the effects of my sin will be reversed. Even though I resisted God's will, He has not rejected me; He has made provision for my forgiveness. And He still has a plan to use my life and make me fruitful. He truly is a redeeming God.

I don't know when or how all His promises will be fulfilled. But I do know that I believe His Word. Whatever days I have left on this earth I want to spend walking in Truth, obeying Him, and influencing those I love to do the same. Believing a lie once brought ruin to my life and family. But now, by the power of His Truth, I have been set free!

❧ FOR FURTHER HELP ❧

I n attempting to give a broad overview of how women to-day are being deceived, we have touched on many difficult and complex issues. You (or someone you know) may be facing one or more of those issues personally. Following is a list of selected re-sources that offer practical help in dealing with specific issues.

To the best of our knowledge, we believe these resources to be true to the Scriptures. However, the inclusion of a resource on this list does not necessarily imply complete agreement with every point or an unqualified endorsement of the author, the resource, or the organization. Every believer should scrutinize all input (including this book) in the light of God's Word.

ABORTION

Her Choice to Heal: Finding Spiritual and Emotional Peace After Abortion, by Sydna Massé and Joan Phillips (Colorado Springs: Chariot Victor, 1998).

Bethany Christian Services, Inc. A national organization whose services include crisis pregnancy and family counseling, infant foster care placement, adoption, and maternity and shepherding homes. 901 Eastern Avenue, N.E., P.O. Box 294, Grand Rapids, MI 49501-0294; 616-224-7610; crisis hot line: 800-BETHANY; www.bethany.org.

Note: Check "Abortion Alternatives" in your *Yellow Pages* for local crisis pregnancy centers.

ADDICTIONS

Addictions: A Banquet in the Grave: Finding Hope in the Power of the Gospel, by Edward T. Welch (Phillipsburg, N.J.: Presbyterian & Reformed, 2001).

Breaking Free: Making Liberty in Christ a Reality in Life, by Beth Moore (Nashville: Broadman & Holman, 2000).

Breaking Free: Making Liberty in Christ a Reality in Life, by Beth Moore (Nashville: LifeWay, 1999). An eleven-week small-group Bible study; available from LifeWay Christian Resources; main switchboard: 615-251-2000, or customer service: 800-458-2772; www.lifewaystores.com.

The Discipline of Grace: God's Role and Our Role in the Pursuit of Holiness, by Jerry Bridges (Colorado Springs: NavPress, 1994). Study guide available.

False Intimacy: Understanding the Struggle of Sexual Addiction, by Dr. Harry W. Schaumburg (Colorado Springs: NavPress, 1997).

What Do You Do When You Know That You Are Hooked? pamphlet by Jay E. Adams (Phillipsburg, N.J.: Presbyterian & Reformed, 1975); www.prpbooks.com.

When People Are Big and God Is Small: Overcoming Peer Pressure, Codependency, and the Fear of Man, by Edward T. Welch (Phillipsburg, N.J.: Presbyterian & Reformed, 1997); www.prpbooks.com.

ASSURANCE OF SALVATION

One Minute After You Die: A Preview of Your Final Destination, by Erwin W. Lutzer (Chicago: Moody, 1997).

Saved Without a Doubt: How to Be Sure of Your Salvation, by John MacArthur, Jr. (Colorado Springs: Chariot Victor, 1992).

CHEMICAL IMBALANCE

Blame It on the Brain? Distinguishing Chemical Imbalances, Brain Disorders, and Disobedience, by Edward T. Welch (Phillipsburg, N.J.: Presbyterian & Reformed, 1998); prpbooks.com.

DEPRESSION

The Journal of Biblical Counseling: Special Issues on Depression, vol. 18, nos. 2, 3. Christian Counseling & Educational Foundation, 1803 East Willow Grove Ave., Glenside, PA 19038; 215-884-7676; e-mail: ccefmail@aol.com; www.ccef.org.

Spiritual Depression: Its Causes and Its Cure, by D. Martyn Lloyd-Jones (Grand Rapids: Eerdmans, 1988).

What Do You Do When You Become Depressed? pamphlet by Jay E. Adams (Phillipsburg, N.J.: Presbyterian & Reformed, 1975); www.prp.com.

DOMESTIC VIOLENCE

The Journal of Biblical Counseling, vol. 15, no. 2 (winter 1997); vol. 16, no. 3 (spring 1998). Christian Counseling & Educational Foundation, 1803 East Willow Grove Ave., Glenside, PA 19038; 215-884-7676; e-mail: ccefmail@aol.com; www.ccef.org.

FOOD/EATING DISORDERS

First Place: Giving Christ First Place, by Carole Lewis with W. Terry Whalin (Ventura, California: Regal Books, a division of Gospel Light, 2001). A program offering materials that focus on the importance of giving Christ first place in all areas of your life, including health issues. The book, *First Place,* and other resources such as Bible studies, audio cassettes, CDs, videos, Scripture memory verses and prayer journals are available through Gospel Light by calling 1-800-4-GOSPEL, or through the web at www.gospel-light.com/firstplace. For information on training opportunities, conferences, rallies, workshops and fitness weeks contact the First Place National Offices in Houston, Texas at 1-800-727-5223, or through the web at www.firstplace.org.

The Journal of Biblical Counseling, Bulimia (vol. 11, no. 2); Anorexia (vol. 11, no. 3). Christian Counseling & Educational Foundation, 1803 East Willow Grove Ave., Glenside, PA 19038; 215-884-7676; e-mail: ccefmail@aol.com; www.ccef.org.

Love to Eat, Hate to Eat: Breaking the Bondage of Destructive Eating Habits, by Elyse Fitzpatrick (Eugene, Oreg.: Harvest House, 1999).

More Than Bread, by Elyse Fitzpatrick (Institute of Biblical Counseling & Discipleship, 1992). A workbook on overeating, bulimia, and anorexia; 619-462-9775.

FORGIVENESS

Forgiveness: Healing the Harbored Hurts of Your Heart, by Bill Elliff (1998). Available from The Summit Church, 6600 Crystal Hill Rd., North Little Rock, AR 72118; 501-758-4822; www.the-summitchuch.org.

I Should Forgive, but . . . : Finding Release from the Bondage of Anger and Bitterness, by Chuck Lynch (Nashville: Word, 1998).

Forgiven, Forgiving, and Free! by Nancy Leigh DeMoss. Audiotape and videotape message; available from Life Action Ministries, 800-321-1538; www.LifeAction.org.

HOMOSEXUALITY

Desires in Conflict: Answering the Struggle for Sexual Identity, by Joe Dallas (Eugene, Oreg.: Harvest House, 1991).

An Ounce of Prevention: Preventing the Homosexual Condition in Today's Youth, by Don Schmierer (Nashville: Word, 1998).

Someone I Love Is Gay: How Family and Friends Can Respond, by Anita Worthen and Bob Davies (Downers Grove, Ill.: InterVarsity, 1996).

Exodus International. A worldwide coalition of Christian ministries that offer support to men and women seeking to overcome homosexuality. P.O. Box 77652, Seattle, WA 98177; 206-784-7799; www.exodusnorthamerica.org.

INFERTILITY/LOSS OF A BABY

The Ache for a Child: Emotional, Spiritual and Ethical Insights for Women Suffering through Infertility and Pregnancy Loss, by Debra Bridwell (Colorado Springs: Chariot Victor, 1994).

The Memories I Cherish, by Sandy Day and Donna Elyea. A devotional journal keepsake to encourage women after the loss of a baby; available from Caleb Ministries, P.O. Box 470093, Charlotte, NC 28247; 704-846-5372; www.calebministries.org.

Morning Will Come, compiled by Sandy Day. An inspirational collection of true stories that offer comfort, hope, and understanding for those who are dealing with infertility, miscarriage, stillbirth, and early infant death; available from Caleb Ministries (see information listed above).

MARRIAGE

Abused? How You Can Find God's Help, workbook by Richard and Lois Klempel (Lima, Ohio: Fairway, 1981).

Biblical Portrait of Marriage: Twelve Life-changing Sessions on Building Biblical Marriages, by Dr. Bruce H. Wilkinson. A video series; available from Walk Thru The Bible Ministries, Inc., 4201 North Peachtree Road, Atlanta, GA 30341; 800-763-5433; www.walkthruthebible.org.

The Excellent Wife: A Biblical Perspective, by Martha Peace (Bemidji, Minn.: Focus, 1997).

The Fruit of Her Hands: Respect and the Christian Woman, by Nancy Wilson (Moscow, Idaho: Canon, 1997).

Hope for the Separated: Wounded Marriages Can Be Healed, by Gary D. Chapman (Chicago: Moody, 1996).

How to Save Your Marriage Alone, by Ed Wheat, M.D. (Grand Rapids: Zondervan, 1983). This practical booklet is a chapter from the book *Love Life for Every Married Couple* (Grand Rapids: Zondervan, 1983).

Lasting Love: How to Avoid Marital Failure, by Alistair Begg (Chicago: Moody, 1997).

Liberated Through Submission, by P. B. Wilson (Eugene, Oreg.: Harvest House, 1997).

Me? Obey Him? The Obedient Wife and God's Way of Happiness and Blessing in the Home, by Elizabeth Rice Handford (Murfreesboro, Tenn.: Sword of the Lord, 1995).

The Power of a Praying Wife, by Stormie Omartian (Eugene, Oreg.: Harvest House, 1997). Prayer and study guide also available.

What Makes a Man Feel Loved: Understanding What Your Husband Really Wants, by Bob Barnes (Eugene, Oreg.: Harvest House, 1998).

MARRIAGE TO A NONBELIEVER

The Prayer Closet Ministries. A network of intercessors who pray for believers who have spouses that are not Christians. Dr. Kevin Meador, 595 Stratton Road, Decatur, MS 39327; 601-635-2180; www.prayerclosetministries.org.

NEW BELIEVER

How to Begin the Christian Life, by George Sweeting (Chicago: Moody, 1993).
Right with God, by John Blanchard (Edinburgh, United Kingdom: Banner of Truth, 1996).

PARENTS

The Tribute and the Promise, by Dennis Rainey (Nashville: Thomas Nelson, 1997). Learn how honoring your parents will bring a blessing to your life.

PARENTING

A Full Quiver: Family Planning and the Lordship of Christ, by Rick and Jan Hess. Self-published. Contact: P.O. Box 974, Brentwood, TN 37024-0974; 866-896-7096; www.quiverfull.com.

Age of Opportunity: A Biblical Guide to Parenting Teens, by Paul David Tripp (Phillipsburg, N.J.: Presbyterian & Reformed, 1997); www.prpbooks.com.

A Mom Just Like You: The Home Schooling Mother, by Vickie and Jayme Farris (Sisters, Oreg.: Loyal Publishing, 2000).

Growing Little Women: Capturing Teachable Moments with Your Daughter, by Donna J. Miller (Chicago: Moody, 1997).

Raising a Christian Daughter in an MTV World, by Mary Ruth Murdoch (Phillipsburg, N.J.: Presbyterian & Reformed, 2000); www.prpbooks.com.

Raising Lambs Among Wolves: How to Protect Your Children from Evil, by Mark I. Bubeck (Chicago: Moody, 1997).

The Power of a Praying Parent, by Stormie Omartian (Eugene, Oreg.: Harvest House, 1995). Prayer and study guide also available.

Shepherding a Child's Heart, 2d ed., by Theodore A. Tripp (Wapwallopen, Pa.: Shepherd, 1998).

Standing on the Promises: A Handbook of Biblical Childrearing, by Douglas J. Wilson (Moscow, Idaho: Canon, 1997).

PORNOGRAPHY

An Affair of the Mind: One Woman's Courageous Battle to Salvage Her Family from the Devastation of Pornography, by Laurie Sharlene Hall (Colorado Springs: Focus on the Family, 1998).

ROLE OF WOMEN

Becoming a Titus 2 Woman, by Martha Peace (Bemidji, Minn.: Focus, 1997).

Biblical Portrait of Womanhood, by Nancy Leigh DeMoss. Booklet available from Life Action Ministries, 800-321-1538; www.LifeAction.org.

Biblical Womanhood in the Home, Nancy Leigh DeMoss, general editor, "Foundations for the Family" series (Wheaton, Ill.: Crossway, 2002).

By Design: God's Distinctive Calling for Women, by Susan Hunt (Wheaton, Ill.: Crossway, 1998).

Fearlessly Feminine: Boldly Living God's Plan for Womanhood, by Jani Ortlund (Sisters, Oreg.: Multnomah, 2000).

Home By Choice, by Brenda Hunter, Ph.D. (Sisters, Oreg.: Multnomah, 1991, 2000).

Leadership for Women in the Church, by Susan Hunt and Peggy Hutcheson (Grand Rapids: Zondervan, 1991).

Let Me Be a Woman, by Elisabeth Elliot (Wheaton, Ill.: Tyndale, 1999).

Portrait of a Foolish Woman: Lessons and Cautions from Proverbs 7. Booklet and/or audiotape, by Nancy Leigh DeMoss; contact: Life Action Ministries, 800 321 1538; www.LifeAction.org.

Portrait of a Woman Used by God: Lessons from the Life of Mary of Nazareth, Booklet and/or audiotape, by Nancy Leigh DeMoss; contact: Life Action Ministries, 800-321-1538; www.LifeAction.org.

Recovering Biblical Manhood and Womanhood: A Response to Evangelical Feminism, edited by John Piper and Wayne A. Grudem (Wheaton, Ill.: Crossway, 1991).

Spiritual Mothering: The Titus 2 Model for Women Mentoring Women, by Susan Hunt (Wheaton, Ill.: Crossway, 1993).

A Woman After God's Own Heart, by Elizabeth George (Eugene, Oreg.: Harvest House, 1997). Practical, scriptural insights on how you can pursue God's priorities concerning your husband, children, home, walk with the Lord, and ministry.

A Woman's High Calling: The 10 Essentials of Godly Living, by Elizabeth George (Eugene, Oreg.: Harvest House, 2001). Explore the essentials of godly living presented in Titus 2:3–5—practical, purposeful advice on living in purity, cultivating discipline, managing a home, loving a husband, and more.

Five Aspects of Woman: A Biblical Theology of Femininity, by Barbara K. Mouser. Twenty-three-lesson textbook with nineteen lectures on audiotape; available through International Center for Gender Studies, P.O. Box 702, Waxahachie, TX 75168; 800-317-6958.

"Wisdom for Women from Titus 2," by Carolyn Mahaney. Eight-tape series; available from PDI Communications, 7881 Beechcraft Ave., Suite B, Gaithersburg, MD 20879-1507; 800-736-2202 or 301-926-2200; e-mail: pdi@pdinet.org; www.pdinet.org.

Council on Biblical Manhood and Womanhood (CBMW). P.O. Box 7337, Libertyville, IL 60048; 847-573-8120; e-mail: info@cbmw.org; www.cbmw.org.

The Proverbs 31 Ministry. Dedicated to providing encouragement and information to women, especially on God's view of homemaking and its responsibilities. Offerings include a monthly newsletter and women's conferences. P.O. Box 17155, Charlotte, NC 28227; 704-849-2270; e-mail: p31home@proverbs31.org; www.proverbs31.org.

SEXUAL ABUSE

Dorie: The Girl Nobody Loved, by Doris Van Stone and Erwin W. Lutzer (Chicago: Moody, 1981). A reminder that God's love, forgiveness, and grace are greater than human hurt and sorrow.

Glenda's Story: Led by Grace, by Glenda Revell (Lincoln, Nebr.: Back to the Bible, 1994). This story of hope is an amazing account of our merciful Savior, who brings light out of darkness, joy out of sorrow, and peace out of pain.

No Place to Cry: The Hurt and Healing of Sexual Abuse, by Doris Van Stone and Erwin W. Lutzer (Chicago: Moody, 1990).

SEXUAL PURITY

And the Bride Wore White: Seven Secrets to Sexual Purity, by Dannah Gresh (Chicago: Moody, 2000).

Forgotten Factors, by Roy Hession (Fort Washington, Pa.: Christian Literature Crusade, 1976).

Intimate Issues: Conversations Woman to Woman: 21 Questions Christian Women Ask About Sex, by Linda Dillow and Lorraine Pintus (Colorado Springs: WaterBrook, 1999).

Passion and Purity: Learning to Bring Your Love Life Under Christ's Control, by Elisabeth Elliot (Grand Rapids: Revell, 1984).

SINGLENESS

The Freedom to Marry: Seven Dynamic Steps to Marriage Readiness, by Ellen Johnson Varughese. Available from JoyPress, P.O. Box 3136, Olathe, KS 66063; 913-829-6555; www.joypress.com.

The Path of Loneliness: It May Seem a Wilderness, but It Can Lead You to God, by Elisabeth Elliot (Nashville: Thomas Nelson, 1991).

The Rich Single Life, by Andrew Farmer (PDI Communications, 1998). Available from PDI Communications, 7881 Beechcraft

Ave., Suite B, Gaithersburg, MD 20879; 800-736-2202 or 301-926-2200; www.pdinet.org.

Singled Out for Him: Embracing the Gift, the Blessings, and the Challenges of Singleness, by Nancy Leigh DeMoss. Available from Life Action Ministries, 800-321-1538; www.LifeAction.org.

Singled Out for Him, by Nancy Leigh DeMoss. Set of three audiotapes; six radio interviews with Dennis Rainey on *FamilyLife Today.* Available from Life Action Ministries, 800-321-1538; www.LifeAction.org.

SUFFERING

Only God Can Heal the Wounded Heart, by Ed Bulkley (Eugene, Oreg.: Harvest House, 1995).

A Path Through Suffering: Discovering the Relationship Between God's Mercy and Our Pain, by Elisabeth Elliot (Ann Arbor, Mich.:Vine, 1992).

Trusting God Even When Life Hurts, by Jerry Bridges (Colorado Springs: NavPress, 1991).

When God Doesn't Make Sense, by Dr. James C. Dobson (Wheaton, Ill.:Tyndale, 1997).

TIME MANAGEMENT

The 15 Minute Organizer, by Emilie Barnes (Eugene, Oreg.: Harvest House, 1991).

The Creative Home Organizer, by Emilie Barnes (Eugene, Oreg.: Harvest House, 1988). Tips and ideas for home organization, food preparation, housecleaning, children, auto care, pets, pests, plants

...and more. Available from More Hours In My Day Ministries (see information below).

More Hours In My Day Ministries. Emilie Barnes conducts "More Hours In My Day" seminars on home management, ministers to those who are suffering from cancer and other traumas of life, and offers books and other resources. Contact: 2838 Whitestone Drive, Riverside, CA 92506; 909-682-4714; e-mail: emilie @emiliebarnes.com; www.emiliebarnes.org.

WOMEN'S ISSUES (MISCELLANEOUS)

Caring for Your Aging Parents: When Love Is Not Enough, by Barbara Deane (Colorado Springs: NavPress, 1989).

In My Father's House: Women Relating to God as Father, by Mary A. Kassian (Nashville: LifeWay, 1999). A six-week interactive study with five daily lessons for individual study and weekly small group sessions; encourages women to clear barriers hindering them from seeing their heavenly Father. Available from LifeWay Christian Resources, 800-458-2722; www.lifewaystores.com.

Women Helping Women: A Biblical Guide to the Major Issues Women Face, edited by Elyse Fitzpatrick and Carol Cornish (Eugene, Oreg.: Harvest House, 1997). Addresses the top twenty concerns women face and offers biblically-based encouragement and practical advice; includes chapters on difficult marriages, infertility, addictions, singleness, rebellious teens, eating disorders, care of dying parents, single moms, and post-abortion women, etc.

❧ NOTES ❧

Chapter 1: Truth . . . or Consequences

1. *Smooth Stones Taken from Ancient Brooks,* comp. Charles H. Spurgeon. (Morgan, Pa.: Soli Deo Gloria, 1996), 93.

Chapter 2: Lies Women Believe . . . About God

1. From the introduction of *The Unselfishness of God;* quoted in *Safe Within Your Love: A Forty-Day Journey in the Company of Hannah W. Smith,* Devotional Readings Arranged and Paraphrased by David Hazard (Minneapolis: Bethany, 1992), 147.
2. Hannah Whitall Smith, *God Is Enough,* ed. Melvin E. Dieter and Hallie A. Dieter (Grand Rapids: Francis Asbury, Zondervan, 1986), 240–41.
3. Hannah Whitall Smith, quoted in *Daily Strength for Daily Needs,* comp. Mary W. Tileston (Boston: Little, Brown, 1899), 333.
4. Smith, *God Is Enough,* 21, 26.

Chapter 3: Lies Women Believe . . . About Themselves

1. "Meg Ryan: What She Really Thinks of Herself," *Ladies' Home Journal,* July 1999, 98.
2. W. E. Vine, *The Expanded Vine's Expository Dictionary of New Testament Words,* ed. John R. Kohlenberger III with James A. Swanson (Minneapolis: Bethany, 1984), 751.

Chapter 4: Lies Women Believe . . . About Sin

1. Amy Bloom, *Self,* April 1999, 40.
2. *The Valley of Vision: A Collection of Puritan Prayers and Devotions,* ed. Arthur Bennett (Carlisle, Pa.: Banner of Truth, 1975), 70, 79.
3. Robert Lowry, "Nothing but the Blood."
4. John Alexander, "And That's That: Sin, Salvation, and Woody Allen," *The Other Side,* January–February 1993, 55.
5. *The Valley of Vision,* 76.

Chapter 5: Lies Women Believe . . . About Priorities

1. Dorothy Patterson, "The High Calling of Wife and Mother in Biblical Perspective," *Recovering Biblical Manhood and Womanhood: A Response to Evangelical Feminishm,* ed. John Piper and Wayne Grudem (Wheaton, Ill.: Crossway, 1991), 365.

2. "An Interview with Kate Hepburn," *Ladies' Home Journal,* March 1977, 54.

3. "Joanne and Paul: Their Lives Together and Apart," *Ladies Home Journal,* July 1975, 62.

4. Patterson, "The High Calling of Wife and Mother in Biblical Perspective," 375.

Chapter 6: Lies Women Believe . . . About Marriage

1. Mary A. Kassian, *The Feminist Gospel: The Movement to Unite Feminism with the Church* (Wheaton, Ill.: Crossway, 1992), 82.

2. Nancy Leigh DeMoss, "Devotion to Family," in *A Mother's Legacy: Wisdom from Mothers to Daughters,* compiled and written by Barbara Rainey and Ashley Rainey Escue (Nashville: Thomas Nelson, 2000), 106–7.

3. *Southern Baptist Convention,* "Baptist Faith and Message," revised June 1998, Article XVIII.

4. Susan Hunt, *The True Woman: The Beauty and Strength of a Godly Woman* (Wheaton, Ill.: Crossway, 1997), 218, 223.

5. For a fuller treatment of the consequences of the Fall as it relates to male/female roles, see Raymond C. Ortlund Jr., "Male-Female Equality and Male Headship: Genesis 1–3," in *Recovering Biblical Manhood and Womanhood: A Response to Evangelical Feminism,* ed. John Piper and Wayne Grudem (Wheaton, Ill.: Crossway, 1991), 95–112.

6. Elizabeth Rice Handford, *Me? Obey Him? The Obedient Wife and God's Way of Happiness and Blessing in the Home* (Murfreesboro, Tenn.: Sword of the Lord, 1994), 75–76.

Chapter 7: Lies Women Believe . . . About Children

1. Shulamith Firestone, *The Dialectic of Sex: The Case for Feminist Revolution* (New York: William Morrow, 1970), 81.

2. Mary Pride, *The Way Home: Beyond Feminism, Back to Reality* (Westchester, Ill.: Crossway, 1985), 77, 75.

3. *The Works of Jonathan Edwards,* with a memoir by Sereno E. Dwight; rev. and corrected by Edward Hickman, 2 vols. (Carlisle, Pa.: The Banner of Truth Trust, 1976), z: 1:xiv.

Chapter 8: Lies Women Believe . . . About Emotions

1. Hannah Whitall Smith, *God Is Enough,* ed. Melvin E. Dieter and Hallie A. Dieter (Grand Rapids: Francis Asbury, Zondervan, 1986), 52–53.

2. Francis de Sales, *Daily Strength for Daily Needs,* ed. Mary W. Tileston (Boston: Little, Brown, 1899), 29.

3. D. Martyn Lloyd-Jones, *Spiritual Depression: Its Causes and Cure* (Grand Rapids: Eerdmans, 1986), 21.

Chapter 9: Lies Women Believe . . . About Circumstances

1. Judith Viorst, *Alexander and the Terrible, Horrible, No Good, Very Bad Day* (New York: Atheneum; Simon & Schuster, 1972).

2. Ibid.

3. Ibid.

4. George Lewis Prentiss, *More Love to Thee: The Life and Letters of Elizabeth Prentiss* (Amityville, N.Y.: Calvary, 1994), 374.

5. Harry C. Green and Mary W. Green, "The Pioneer Mothers of America," 1912, cited in *The Christian History of the American Revolution: Consider and Ponder,* comp. Verna M. Hall (San Francisco: Foundation of American Christian Education, 1988), 76.

6. R. Arthur Mathews, *Ready for Battle: 31 Studies in Christian Discipleship* (Wheaton, Ill.: Harold Shaw, 1993), 123, 71.

7. William Law, cited in *Daily Strength for Daily Needs,* ed. Mary W. Tileston (Boston: Little, Brown, 1899), 17.

8. Hannah Whitall Smith, *God Is Enough,* ed. Melvin E. Dieter and Hallie A. Dieter (Grand Rapids: Francis Asbury, Zondervan, 1986), 132.

9. Larry Crabb, *Finding God* (Grand Rapids: Zondervan, 1993), 17–18.

10. Frances R. Havergal, "Like a River Glorious."

11. Susan Hunt, *The True Woman* (Wheaton, Ill.: Crossway, 1997), 75.

Nancy Leigh DeMoss is an author, conference speaker, and the host of *Revive Our Hearts,* a daily radio program for women heard on over 230 stations nationwide. She has also produced numerous booklets, audiotapes, and videotapes to promote personal and corporate revival, and to help women cultivate a more intimate relationship with God.

For more information about *Revive Our Hearts* and other available resources, contact:

> Revive Our Hearts
> P.O. Box 31
> Buchanan, MI 49107-0031
>
> (269) 684-5905; (269) 684-0923 (fax);
> E-mail: ReviveOurHearts@LifeAction.org
> www.ReviveOurHearts.com

Revive Our Hearts is an outreach of Life Action Ministries.

Revive Our Hearts Radio is a ministry partnership of Back to the Bible, FamilyLife Today, and Life Action Ministries.

A Place of Quiet Rest

Finding Intimacy with God through a Daily Devotional Life

Have you found yourself fighting to make daily time with your Lord a consistent reality?

Author Nancy Leigh DeMoss shares from her heart and life how a daily devotional time can forever change your relationship with Jesus. She addresses common frustrations and pitfalls that most of us encounter in our devotional life, and makes practical suggestions for overcoming them.

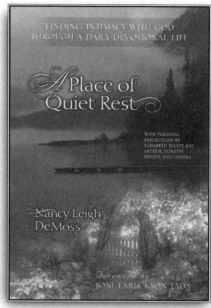

ISBN: 0-8024-6643-5

A 30-Day Walk With God in the Psalms

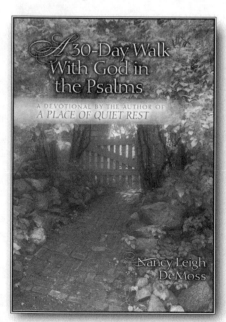

Would you like to develop a meaningful daily quiet time?

Without a doubt, one of the most significant influences in the life of Nancy Leigh DeMoss was the example of parents who practiced the spiritual discipline of a daily devotional life.

For author Nancy Leigh DeMoss the habit of setting aside time alone with the Lord each day has become a nothing less than a necessity -- a key to cultivating intimacy with God. And to the degree you make this your daily focus, you too will experience great freedom, joy and blessing.

ISBN: 0-8024-6644-3

Walking in the Truth

The Companion Guide for Lies Women Believe

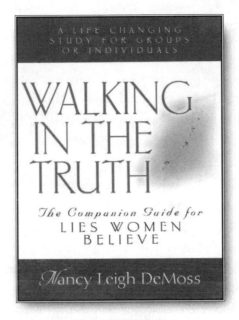

ISBN: 0-8024-4692-2

Now here is a resource that will help you go deeper with the truths from Nancy's best-selling book *Lies Women Believe*. These penetrating questions will make you and your friends think and wrestle with the Truth as you search the Word for answers to tough issues. Truth is not just something to know but something to live out in the laboratory of life as you apply the Word to real-life situations. *Walking in the Truth* is ideal for small groups, Bible studies and Sunday school classes.

MOODY
PUBLISHERS
THE NAME YOU CAN TRUST.

1-800-678-6928 www.MoodyPublishers.com

Sɪɴᴄᴇ 1894, Moody Publishers has been dedicated to equip and motivate people to advance the cause of Christ by publishing evangelical Christian literature and other media for all ages, around the world. Because we are a ministry of the Moody Bible Institute of Chicago, a portion of the proceeds from the sale of this book go to train the next generation of Christian leaders.

If we may serve you in any way in your spiritual journey toward understanding Christ and the Christian life, please contact us at www.moodypublishers.com.

"All Scripture is God-breathed and is useful for teaching, rebuking, correcting and training in righteousness, so that the man of God may be thoroughly equipped for every good work."
—2 Timothy 3:16, 17

MOODY
PUBLISHERS

THE NAME YOU CAN TRUST®